HOW TO MONETIZE YOUTUBE VIDEOS

Youtube secrets for beginners, Youtube marketing & algorithms & Instagram power usage. Guide YouTubers How to Vlog Like a Pro and Become the Best Social Media Influencers

Donall Kargard

Contents

I

<u>Before we begin</u>

YouTube is the second most visited page globally and a phenomenal tool to generate passive income online. Today, becoming a YouTuber is a hot trend and a job opportunity for many young people. However, it is not so simple to earn money on YouTube. The platform's popularity has given rise to competition, and you may always find someone doing something better than you do, but that is not the case for having success.

Earning money with YouTube is not so complicated because you have a ton of opportunities to generate income. There are millions of people trying to find a place on this platform. For most famous YouTubers, the primary source of income is the external collaborations they make with the brands, and not from the views that their videos have.

A lot of things need to be streamlined for your channel to be profitable. And even more now, because the platform recently changed its advertising policy: currently 10,000 visits are necessary on a channel to start entering money for advertising. This book is not the get-rich-quick scheme that you can find over the Internet because trust me, all of that's rubbish. It is not a quick fix or the insane hack to generate passive income.

We are talking about actionable strategies, methods that will require you to push boundaries, and facts which may not sound nice to you. However, I genuinely believe that you deserve every truth regarding monetization on YouTube, which will help you make the right choices and be successful.

We will explore the myriads of opportunities at YouTube's disposal, smart strategies, case studies, and examples of some of the most prominent YouTubers that the world's crazy for. We will uncover the nitty-gritty details and answers to some of the most complicated questions in this domain. Above all, we will prove the value of this eBook by the time you are done reading. The pros and cons of having a YouTube channel are part of a topic that deserves to be addressed.

Especially since many expect optimal results after the creation of a channel, but they do not know all the work that its maintenance requires to achieve good numbers. Being a YouTuber is becoming more and more fashionable.

It allows you to access a global and alternative audience by creating creative content. Justin Bieber was a YouTube star before launching as a musician. Everyone knows PewDiePie. He is one of the biggest and mainstream YouTubers with more than 100 million subscribers and has earned millions of dollars with his content on the platform.

And they are not the only ones. Lilly Singh, Dude Comedy, David Dobrick, James Charles are some of the well-known faces on YouTube who have managed to monetize their content and earn millions of dollars. But like any other content strategy, it requires time, work, and perseverance.

Possibilities With YouTube Are Promising and Realistic

YouTube is one of the leading social media networks. It is an excellent source of entertainment that can range from movies to television shows to marketing videos to fun content of all kinds. Creating a YouTube channel can help you and your business venture interact with specific audiences in a unique and personal way. And although it may take time to produce video content, the result will be worth it. What should you consider before starting? These are seven advantages that you can get if you choose to open a YouTube channel:

You can upload almost any type of video

There are not many restrictions on the types of videos you can upload to your YouTube channel. This factor gives you the freedom to expand on what you like best among the pros and cons of having a YouTube channel. Besides, you can also point out the different videos that you think are more interesting on your channel.

You can include links to your website

Include links to your site on YouTube or to the landing page that you see appropriate. Without a doubt, it is not necessary to tell you how to classify this option among the pros and cons of having a YouTube channel.

Deriving qualified traffic to your landing page will always be an affirmative action. These links act as internal organic links that are used for SEO purposes. But this, in turn, will help promote your website. Google also loves to promote things that can be found in its own products, which will give you another natural boost.

Starting on YouTube does not cost money

If your marketing budget is minimal or you need to adjust it, you have good news. You don't have to pay anything to get started in this world. Although you will need to invest some money in resources to create compelling video content that can succeed.

The videos you upload to your channel can be embedded

YouTube embedded videos: one of the most significant benefits of starting with a YouTube channel is how videos can be shared. You can allow others to insert your video on their website to obtain additional visits. And there are even options to change the content size or frame color by embedding it.

It is a perfect channel for branding

Among the pros and cons of having a YouTube channel, it should be noted that this is the ideal ally for your brand; precisely to do branding. The concept of making a brand should be understood as creating a community, working on the user's perception of your company when they hear about it, etc.

The use of YouTube for digital marketing strategies should focus precisely on working and squeezing the brand's identity. Something that is not only achieved by selling a product, or with a profit account. Many times, more intangible elements are used.

21st-century users are tired of promotions and are looking for much more personal communication with brands. They hope that they become humanized. Sometimes this communication can be unprofessional by specific standards, but it is what is worked. Closeness, imperfection, and almost anecdotal triumph on YouTube works.

Another factor that you must take into account to do branding on this platform is to analyze whether other people or brands in your domain are on YouTube or not. If you have dared to jump into the pool, your brand could be the pioneer on this platform.

It allows you to work on your passion

Among the pros and cons of having a YouTube channel, you cannot overlook the most personal and enriching advantage of all: your satisfaction. Unless you're working for National Geographic or Discovery, office jobs are routine and can be tedious and demotivating.

Whether you are a writer, producer, entertainer, or director, YouTube gives you the option to follow your passion and unleash your creativity. Do you have an idea? All you have to do is write a script, produce the content yourself, and share it. Ka-boom! YouTube's career is not based solely on earning a fixed salary.

It's about finding your audience, making it vibrate with you while you follow your passion. It lets you connect with strangers and share your passion with them, regardless of where they are in the world.

You do not need degrees or minimum age to succeed

Perhaps you do not know how to catalog this idea among the pros and cons of having a YouTube channel. But remember that you have complete freedom to choose which content to upload, which to edit, and set your own pace is always positive.

In short, you will be your own boss. You only need talent and the best practices to monetize it in the future.

Some funding is needed to drive ideas that require a little more production.

Recording and editing videos from smartphones are possible. And the result is probably better than you expect. But if you are looking to differentiate yourself by your video content, you need a decent team and equipment. So, if you are interested in producing high-quality content, you will have to invest in it.

You need to be constant to achieve results

YouTube has billions of makeup tutorials, which use high-end products. If you want to stand out, you need to have a fixed audience, a robust, faithful community. And for this, there is nothing like having a strict schedule that you commit to.

For example, an editorial calendar that helps you monitor and streamline the frequency of content launch. Creating YouTubes videos consistently with top-notch quality is a significant challenge. It can be said that the first challenge would be to create the correct script for each one.

Achieving results takes time

Viral videos are from another world. It is difficult to detect which element has led to content going viral. Even if your content is focused on the latest trends, it's hard to find a whole audience that echoes your content so much. Three hundred hours of content is uploaded each every minute. Therefore, it is complicated to be among the 5 billion videos that are seen every day on the platform.

Cultivating an organic audience of hundreds of thousands of viewers can take time. This does not classify the idea as one of the pros or cons of having a YouTube channel. You just need to know that the results do not come overnight.

Without perseverance, effort, and patience, you will not get good results.

Ideas are constantly copied

Launching your YouTube channel is fairly simple. But what if your intellectual property is stolen, and the stolen ideas find a kickass momentum you couldn't? Many brands aggressively pursue plagiarism, but newbie players can't track content uploaded regularly, so it is impossible to find out if content was copied.

YouTube channels inevitably highlight the videos of your competition

YouTube is aimed at providing users with videos that best suit their preferences. This is how advertising revenue is generated. That means that all the competing videos will be shown while the user is consuming your video.

There are no guarantees that your videos will be viewed

There are some videos on YouTube that have more than 4 billion views. But some do not even reach 50 meager views. Just because you've launched yourself into creating a YouTube channel doesn't mean you're automatically going to draw attention to your content. As with any Internet channel, you must promote your content on other channels so that your target can find you.

All in all, despite the pros and cons of having a YouTube channel, taking advantage of this platform is no longer a mystery. YouTube has a high rate of visits, and precisely those visits are the basis to start earning money with a YouTube channel. Don't waste time and start earning money with a YouTube channel!

Knowing how to get started on YouTube is not a difficult thing. Opening a channel is a process that only takes a few minutes and where the most complicated part is finding original YouTube names that also meet individual requirements: they must be easy to remember, not look like any that already exist, and also be free both on the Google video platform and in other corners of the Internet; since sooner or later it could be interesting to buy a domain or register on various social networks.

Once the name that best represents us has been chosen, the bureaucratic moment of creating the channel arrives. Following the steps is simple: just reach the "Login" button in the top-right edge and select "Create account".

So, we will get to the Google form with which the company gives access to its entire ecosystem. But it doesn't end there. Now is the time to personalize the channel: you will need a description that summarizes the theme in 1,000 characters, a profile image, and, even more importantly – a header for your channel. For the latter, you need a 2560x1440 YouTube cover that weighs no more than 6 megabytes.

If you don't know much about design, don't suffer; there are many free templates to start on YouTube on the Internet. A quick Google search would do you good. Now comes the challenging part.

Not surprisingly, there is no foolproof formula that tells how to be successful on YouTube. There's no insane recipe that anyone can sell you for a few hundred dollars. Those seminars are not worth it either. There are some steps that you can follow in your first moments on the platform to have a good start.

It is one of the great unknowns that many of those who want to follow the path of their idols on YouTube ask themselves: what do I do on the channel? To start answering that question, forget what you've seen before and the YouTubers you regularly follow; you're in danger of being an unoriginal content creator. Be original. Bring your own product.

What is it that you do? Do not imitate anyone out there. Yeah, PewDiePie plays Minecraft all the time, but do you have to walk the same route?

You will not be known for it.

When opting for one of the infinite themes to make YouTube videos, keep in mind that the platform was born in 2005 and that more than 5 billion videos have been uploaded in it. In this context, it is difficult for a YouTuberto start his career in 2020 and do so by finding a topic that has not been previously addressed.

There are even channels dedicated to the breeding of ants with half a million video views. Those who want to take their first steps will have to look for their differential factor in other aspects. Do you want to be a YouTuber gamer? Try beauty products? Podcasts? Make educational art history animated content? Do tutorials? DIY projects? Roast people? Plane spotting?

Choose what you like best, but try to make videos which have a new approach, either when it comes to addressing the topic or editing the videos themselves. Whatever you choose, meditate well before launching and, above all, opt for something you like and with which you are comfortable.

Remember that your medium-term goal is for your channel to become your job. Once this decision has been made, and the first video recorded, the steps to upload a video to YouTube are simple. In the top-right edge, you will find see the icon (an arrow pointing up).

After clicking, select the video you are going to upload, and while it is being processed, pay close attention to the following screen: on it, you will have to put a title, description, and labels. In addition to summarizing the video's content, you should choose the keywords well so that, in addition to the views of your future subscribers, you receive visits from other users who are looking for something on your topic.

Finally, before publishing the first video of your channel, you will have to choose a thumbnail. It is very essential and it is more than a mere title. It should be eye-catching and if it has lyrics, they should be easy to see, but keep in mind that excess is not usually good.

The most striking YouTube thumbnails do not have to be the ones that contain the most visual stimuli. Sometimes it is more profitable to bet on the simple. When creating the thumbnail, there are several options.

On one hand, you can select the ones suggested by the platform itself when you have already uploaded the video. It probably won't be the best alternative. If you want to design your own miniature, you can choose to do it with Photoshop if you have the program and know how to use it or opt for the most straightforward and most complete free alternative.

"I Need to Contact YouTube. What Do I Do?"

Whether as a simple user or as an active member of the community, there are times when you will need to contact YouTube. And if you don't know where to start for that, this eBook aims to help you out and condense, in one place, all the ways you have to get in touch with the world's most popular Video Social Network YouTube.

Directly on the YouTube Help Center, the user can find a multitude of answers that they have about YouTube and its policies, operation, etc. You will only have to describe your problem and, if it is solved, it will appear in the predictive text.

You can also leave your query in the official forum of the YouTube community or visit the official channel of help videos that the social network makes available to all users. That's a win.

If you want to report a security problem (computer attacks, for example, that you personally detect) in the YouTube community, you must do so by writing in the search box that says, "Describe your issue."

The general YouTube contact email is generalinfo@youtube.com; if you want to contact them directly due to account suspension or any other problem. If you are or want to be a creator on YouTube, you can find all information about it on YouTube dot com/creators.

If someone is infringing copyright, you can report it by writing your issue on the dialogue box. You should contact YouTube through the Policies and Safety portal if you have suffered or are a witness to any abuse in the social network. If you want to directly reach out to YouTube headquarters in the United States or send mail, here's the official address:

YouTube, LLC

901 Cherry Ave.

San Bruno, CA 94066

USA

Fax: +1 650-253-0001

By the end of this, you will know all about monetizationon YouTube in 2020. More specifically, this book will tell you how much money YouTube earns and how much is earned by each subscriber and visit on YouTube, and how it is done to earn money by uploading videos to

YouTube.

Also, I will give you actionable insights so that your videos receive more visits, and we will explain how to gain subscribers on YouTube.

YouTube Partner Program (YPP)

The easiest way is to upload videos to YouTube and earn money from the content created. But this has nuances. If you want to monetize videos, you must know how the YouTube Partner Program works in 2020.

Monetization is unavailable until a channelsigns up for YouTube Partner Program or YPP. Once your channel reaches 1,000 subscribers and 4,000 hours of public playtime, can it be eligible to join YPP.

You are unable to generate income on YouTube until you meet the threshold. So, it is essential to create content consistently and maximize reach of your channel.

Now that you are aware of how many visits you have to have on YouTube to earn money, let's answer other frequently asked questions from users. "How much do you get paid on YouTube? How much are a million views on YouTube worth?"

There is no exact figure that can estimate what you will earn with a million views on YouTube. This platform does not pay as per the number of visits but offers a commission for other complementary actions: advertising, Superchat, memberships, etc.

This implies that the greater the number of visits, the more way you can secure options for the financial compensation you can capitalize on. In a general view, if your content is top-of-the-line, the community will relate to your content. It will sway their opinions and will likely subscribe to your channel. This will, in effect, help your channel to generate advertising income. More companies want to offer you compensation in exchange for promoting their products.

Visits are not the only thing you should be concerned about. Read on to understand how you can make money with YouTube via the channel of Advertising.

YouTube does not pay based on the number of subscribers you have. This figure is only important to get an idea of the money that can be earned on YouTube through advertising revenue, affiliate marketing, Superchat, membership, merchandising, collaborations, etc., as we mentioned previously. Although there are tools that estimate the income of influencers, the truth is that there is no exact way to know how much a YouTuber earns.

Their main income comes from contracts/collaborations with companies (private contracts, of course), affiliation commissions, advertising, etc. As it may seem logical, the bigger your channel and your community, the more income they will have, but their final compensation also depends on which ways they manage to monetize their content, making it impossible to know for sure how much money you earn with YouTube.

YouTube Partner Program (YPP) Facts, Eligibility, and Complete Overview
YPP provides creators with access to the platform's bunch of features and resources. Let's overview the available features, and terms for joining, a list of tasks to apply to participate, and some frequently asked questions. YouTube Partner Program offers you:

- Creator Support Teams access

- Copyright Match Tool access

- Monetization Functions access

Minimum eligibility terms to join are a total of five. First of all, each user must comply with all YouTube monetization policies. YouTube's monetization policies bring rules that enable creators to monetize videos.

If you sign with YPP, your agreement containing the YouTube Partner Program policies proposes that you comply with the terms to monetize videos. Secondly, you must reside in a region where YPP is enabled.

Your channel must amass over 4,000 valid public playback hours in the last one year. In addition, you must earn over 1,000 subscribers and a linked AdSense account.

A To-Do List for YouTube Partner Program Application
Channels that clear the required threshold can apply to participate in the YPP, but they must also meet some of the guidelines before they could consider it. Ensure that your channel complies with YouTube's guidelines and policies.

When you submit your request, a standard review process will be applied to your channel to verify that it meets the platform's guidelines and policies. Only channels that reflect such compliance will be accepted into the program. YouTube also continually reviews the program's channels to ensure that they remain in order.

To evaluate channels to consider your participation in the YouTube Partner Program, you need to have content. Usually, creators meet this criterion because they already have content uploaded.

The subscriber criteria and hours help YouTube operators asses and come to a better-informed decision regarding whether your channel is compatible.

Creators only apply to the YPP after reaching the threshold. You can request the operators to notify when you reach the required number of subscribers and public replay hours. When your channel reaches the terms, do the following: Access YouTube.

On right, navigate on the profile picture> YouTube Studio. On left, click Monetization. If you still don't reach the required threshold, click on "Notify me when I'm eligible..." Otherwise, click Get Started on the "See Partner Program Terms" card. When you accept them, the operator will mark this step as "Done" in green on the card.

Ensure you only have a single AdSense account. You will need to connect your AdSense account to receive payments. On the "Sign up for Google AdSense" card, click Start. Use AdSense account that is already approved. Link your channels if you want one AdSense account. When you have connected your AdSense account, the operator will mark this step as "Done" in green on the "Sign up for Google AdSense" card. Wait for the review.

Once YPP terms are agreed and connected to an AdSense account, your channel will automatically enter a review row. YouTube's automated systems and manual reviewers will examine channel content to verify that it meets all of our guidelines.

You can view the status of the application at any time. If the operator accepts you at the YPP: Bingo, time to dance! Now you can configure ad preferences and enable monetization on uploads.

If the operator does not accept you at YPP: the reviewers determined that a significant part of your channel does not comply with YouTube's policies and guidelines. Sorry about that.

You can resubmit a request 30 days after the rejection of your incorporation. Review YouTube's FAQ section and get suggestions to improve your application. You got this!

When you reach the subscriber and playtime thresholds, agree to the YouTube Partner Program Terms, and connect to an AdSense account, your entry request will go into one row. The network's manual reviewers will evaluate your entire channel to see if it complies with YouTube's Monetization Policies.

You will be contacted to inform of the decision once the operator has reviewed your channel (it's a month after you reach the required threshold, so hold your horses). Occasionally, you may have to wait for more than a month.

Delays can have various causes, such as higher than normal request volume, system problems, or occasional resource changes. YouTube's operators try to review applications as soon as possible, but delays can occur due to the amount of applications in queue.

This is way too much to process, I understand. How can we speed up the processing of your application? Well, there's no way you can do that. The teams cannot speed up the process. All requests are aligned in a row and assessed in order of receipt.

Sometimes channels need more scrutiny, especially when there are discrepancies between different reviewers regarding a channel's compatibility for YPP. It can follow multiple reviews in process which means more delays.

Advertising on YouTube – the game changer

If you want to make a YouTube channel and earn money, the first option is to take advantage of the income you will receive from advertising, which will vary depending how many times ads are viewed by users.

This means that your number of subscribers will not determine your final profit, but it will give you a good idea of how much is earned by advertising on YouTube. The money you earn on YouTube for displaying advertising depends on: The type of ad (banner, discovery, whether or not it can be skipped, etc.).

However, you cannot decide what kind of ad will be shown on your channel or its content. Playtime is vital, don't forget. Competitiveness:Ads on YouTube work by bidding, so you'll earn more money with larger advertisers or competing for a more saturated niche.

It is important to mention that as a content creator, you have no control over the ads beyond choosing when they can be displayed. YouTube and its algorithm are in charge of making the necessary optimizations to show relevant ads to an interested audience.

Companies are aware of the potential that social networks have, so they are always interested in finding influencers to promote their products. Once you get enough subscribers and visits, these companies are likely to ask you to advertise or promote their services products via your videos in exchange for compensations.

This can be an excellent way to sponsor videos and advertise products that viewersare interested in and generate additional revenue.However, be careful in doing so; viewers are very susceptible to ads and promotions.

Bonus tip: only promote products that interest you and that you consider suitable for your niche. That will keep your faithful viewers happy. In addition to sporadic collaborations, many companies may also offer to join their affiliate program.

This means that for each person who registers on their platform through a unique link that they will create for you, you will receive a commission. Undoubtedly, affiliate marketing is one of the marketing actions that we see the most among companies.

So even if you have a small audience or want to start in this world, research online which companies (related to your niche) have this program and may be interested in you being a part of it.

You can also make money by a make-shift YouTube online store. It doesn't matter if you already have a successful e-commerce business. There are many ways to sell products online, and making a YouTube channel to earn money is one of them.

Let's explain it a little more in-depth. Let's say you want to make your way in e-commerce and are looking for alternative ways to get more sales; YouTube is an excellent platform to do so. There are many advantages of making videos on YouTube to grow your brand, so we have created some points with the most important ones. Gain brand visibility:Using YouTube to grow your business will undoubtedly help you increase your brand's reach.

I have already said that YouTube is the leading search engine after Google, so with its platform, you will have access to a broad audience.

Surely after the publication of some videos, many of your new customers will come from this social network. Don't forget to analyze your income on YouTube, in order to prioritize your budget when planning your marketing strategies. Show that your brand is professional. Earning money with YouTube by uploading videos is not the only way to take advantage of this platform. Besides, it will help you demonstrate that your branding strategy is professional and legitimate. By creating engaging video content, your viewers (and leads) will associate that content with your brand. And it will give them more confidence in your products.

Humanize your brand: You can also use YouTube to show the people behind your brand and make it more human. If your customers know you, they will be more likely to purchase in your online store. They will also connect with you on a individualand personal note since you will engage with them directly on topics that interest them. So, read on to find out everything you need to be a Youtuber and earn money.

Recycle your content:One of the advantages of investing your efforts in earning money with YouTube is that you are offering your users a new way to access your content. Content marketing is impeccable for growing your business, but blogs are becoming less popular. But if you are still interested, then, without doubt, the best Content Management System (CMS) is WordPress.

If you also create content on a blog, you will be accessing a whole new audience. So, if you already have any gig going on, go ahead, promote your platform and your products/services both in videos and descriptions. It is an excellent way to drive traffic to your blog.

To make money with YouTube, your videos must receive many visits. Here are some insights on

16

making your content one of the most viewed on YouTube: Create engaging and informative content. Users are crazy aboutentertaining videos or which contain valuable information.

If are able to provide your audience with quality video content, they are likely to stick around for the full length of video and return in the future, which is vital to making money on YouTube by uploading videos. Publish regularly and consistently. The great advice I give to anyone who asks how to make a YouTube channel and earn money is 'consistency'.

Not only will the YouTube algorithm benefit you, but it's good for creating a stronger relationship with your audience. When are consistent with a flow of content for viewers, they will continue to interact with you.

They are likely to be much aware of your channel. It is also crucial that you pay attention to the best times to publish your content to take advantage of when people are most likely to see your videos, which will help new users discover your channel. This means doing a little Google research and getting familiar with Google Analytics.

The platform will reveal the most trusted data and numbers on what's happening, what's selling, what's not selling, what's great, what's awful, and where do you stand? Even if you are scared of Math, Google Analytics is very friendly and fun.

Collaborate with other creators YouTubers: One strategy to earn money from YouTube videos is to collaboration.

Thisexcellent method will lead to increasingreach of your channel, offer unique content, and reach your content to a broader audience. Do some research on the YouTubers that are popular in your target market and get in touch with them; they are likely to collaborate. It is very similar to influencer marketing on Instagram only on YouTube. You can pitch ideas to other content creators.

A good option is to DM them or attend events where you may run into the likes of Marques Brownlee and others. And if you see Logan Paul, best ignore. Try to make your videos last more than 10 minutes: YouTube videos longer than 10 minutes have a longer playing time, which contributes positively to advertising revenue generated.

Plus, videoswithmore average playtime will rank better in search engines. In short, posting longer videos will earn you more money with YouTube

Try to create attractive thumbnails and video titles that call the click. When you create a YouTube channel, there will be a large community of YouTubers who will fight for your audience's attention. It is essential to keep be mindful of these factors when making content. And above all, when promoting it:

DO   NOT   CLICKBAIT.

I cannot stress this enough. Clickbait is not a tactic or strategy. It is malpractice, and this book highly discourages you from adopting this practice.

On the other hand, you must not forget that YouTube is a very visually oriented site, so making attractive designs will help you attract more users and consequently, earn more money on YouTube. Also, make sure that the audio and video quality of your content is professional. Audio and video quality must be top-notch. Needless to say, this also plays an important role in your success. You must present your brand positively and professionally, so your video content must be of high quality. Today, thanks to technology, this does not mean that you have to invest a lot. Many mobile video editing apps can be of great help to you.

Say hello to Adobe Premiere Pro. Don't forget about the importance of SEO on YouTube. You can also make more money with YouTube taking care of the SEO of your videos, especially in descriptions and titles. Without a doubt, it is a cray way to drive organic web traffic to your YouTube channel.

The reality of making money on YouTube by uploading videos

Many users are surprised to see what YouTubers really earn. Undoubtedly, making money with videos on YouTube is possible, but you will need to get many visits and subscribers first. If you think a good way to make money is by uploading videos quickly, I am afraid I have bad news. Of course, generating income on YouTube has its limitations.

However, you should think about what other things it can bring to you and your brand: visibility, gifts, contacts, etc. Making videos for money may not be the best way to monetize your efforts, but that doesn't mean you can't make money on YouTube.

Even so, you can, and take advantage of all the resources of this platform to offer your users more visual and user-friendly content. It can help you build brand confidence by displaying your products or even loyalty to your customers if you decide to give a discount coupon to your subscribers, for example.

"I Wanna Retire Jeff Bezos. What Else Can I Do?"

Alternatives to making money with YouTube: Drop shipping. Another revenue generating model is drop shipping. Drop shipping allows entrepreneurs to manage their e-commerce stores without having an inventory.

If you have a drop shipping venture, simply connect with your suppliers every time you receive an order, and they will dispatch products directly to your customers. You can have a drop shipping ventured operated globally and anywhere on the planet. It is effortless to start your own drop shipping store.

Shopify is the most popular option. You can set up your online store in less than 30 minutes and start drops hipping today. If you are interested, give it a try. It's free and ridiculously cool.

II

An overview of reaching your target audience on YouTube

Content creators are beginning to realize YouTube's potential to reach new and hard-to-reach audiences just by changing their concept of creating and distributing content. A revolution is taking place in the living rooms of every home.

We continue to enjoy the content that entertains and stimulates us, but multimedia consumption habits are changing dramatically, especially for users between the ages of 16 and 34.

This change is due to two trends that go hand in hand: users are increasingly searching for content on the Internet and mobile devices are becoming the key means of accessing this content. Currently, more than half of YouTube views are made from smartphones.

Viewers want content related to their hobbies and presented by people who convey credibility and warmth. Some innovative content creators are increasing and developing concepts that span all sorts of interests - from music and humor to sports and cooking; you name it!

Media companies and their advertising partners have increasing opportunities to use YouTube and collaborate with this new generation of creators to increase their coverage and engage with the youth demographic, which is difficult to reach. This YouTube-born talent can draw huge fan communities to the mainstream media and appeal to a whole new audience.

For example, humorist and writer 'Grace Helbig' has garnered nearly 3 million subscribers to her YouTube channel following the success of her 'My Damn Channel' web series. Now she presents her television program, 'The Grace Helbig Show, on E!' and attributes her influence on the "incredibly strong" connection she maintains with her audience.

At a more strategic level, media brands like Radio 1 and Buzzfeed are doing well after focusing their operations on YouTube.

They are taking advantage of the opportunities offered by this platform in terms of creativity, distribution, and audience data to create stronger audiences. Frank Cooper, Buzzfeed Marketing, and Creative Director summarize his strategy as "create, distribute, learn and iterate."

One of the main advantages of YouTube is the speed with which you know your target audience's opinion. This allows creators to establish a culture in which this data is quickly incorporated into the creative process, and the expectations of the audience are met.

With two million subscribers, Radio 1 is the most successful radio station on YouTube. Although broadcasting radio through a video platform seems somewhat contradictory, the station researched to determine how and where their target demographic was spending time, and the result, as expected, was that they were engaged in watching videos on devices.

To help you not waste your budget and resources, here are my recommendations for designing a YouTube strategy:

- Listen to your audience, consult their comments, and act accordingly.

- Make sure that the production quality lives up to the expectations of the audience (that is neither too low nor too high).

- Plan a constant distribution of content instead of publishing content sporadically.

- Collect and use data from your audience (a wealth of relevant information is available, including when and how they view content and from what devices).

- Be sure to post the right content at the right time.

Buzzfeed's Cooper says, "Art and science now play an equally important role in creating quality content." Creators that bring together a team of creative talents, researchers, developers, data analysts, and data professionals to create and distribute videos will have a clear advantage in keeping your content relevant and increasing your income.

Marketing YouTube videos for a creator or small business is one of the most efficient guerrilla weapons you can use to attract customers via the Internet.

Now is the time to consider using this medium to publicize your products or services effectively and with little competition compared to the text. Why should you upload videos to YouTube from your company? Here, I'll give you my reasons because there are many more.

You must not forget that people love videos. They are literally obsessed with visual content. It's not my observation after watching my dad spend every afternoon watching impeachment videos and chugging on Tomi Lahren's far-right cocktails.

A glimpse at greater possibilities

YouTube hosts 90 % of Internet video viewing. More than 80% of people who consume content on the Internet prefer video over blogs. Most of us are visual. 7 out of 10 Internet users in the United States consume YouTube videos frequently.

Videos are 50 times more likely to position themselves in Google results as there is less competition and less professionalism. When they want to learn to do something (computer, kitchen, etc.), most people turn to YouTube.

Interesting if you want to add value online to attract potential customers. And, let's not forget that it is much more effective. The effectiveness of the videos is more than evident if we consider the Cone of Experience (Pyramid of Learning) by Edgar Dale. Yeah, science b!@$%*.

This explains to you that people retain 50% of what we see and hear in our memory while only 10% of what we read. Therefore, if you do video marketing for your tutorials, you are five times more efficient in your "reader's" mind than if you only used written articles. If your business is within teaching instruction, it is the most effective way to share your knowledge.

When I have to learn something, the first thing I turn to is YouTube. Sorry, Skillshare. It is one of my main sources of knowledge after books. Or haven't you heard the phrase? "YouTube it!" Now let's add more credibility.

Making videos while showing your face is the most effective tool to gain your potential clients' credibility since you will quickly position yourself as a benchmark in your market.

We are programmed to recognize greater authority for those familiar to us, so appearing in a video will eventually shorten distances. Of course, you have to offer quality videos and show your face in them.

Nothing to hide behind a logo. At first, you will be unknown to everyone, but little by little, you will see how they become familiar with your face and recognize you. Did I mention it is relatively cheap? This matter is very relative if we consider the type of video we want to make. When I talk about prices, I mean the price of diffusion: how to get it to many people, although it is likely that you will have to go through the cash register to pay the platform. If you get quantifiable results, of course, do not think much about it and pay.

I have known people who paid fairly to YouTube, but I understand that there may be a lot of competition in some sectors, and it is necessary to build a portfolio. Of course, you can upload them to YouTube for free and share it in social networks or on your website.

Put a link to your video as in the signature of your emails. Present them to a customer. Countless occasions to make people watch your videos. Yeah, be that annoying uncle or cousin.

As for the complexity of spending on the video, that will have to be decided by your pocket and what you want to spend on them. We will come to that later. You can make videos with a simple smartphone or webcam on your computer.

Do a little touch up with free programs and upload them. It's that simple and cheap. But that's only to get started with. Once you are going full throttle, then you will need to invest in pro equipment and software.

You can also leverage greater visibility. Come to think of it; YouTube is massive – a complete universe.

This means that the visibility you can have with a good video is immense. What's more, I would dare to say that it is great considering the little competition of videos that exist in many sectors. In fact, on YouTube, there are many jokes and laughs and rants, but there are not so many serious videos and providing value and solutions to problems.

Also, if you know how to segment well and your market is very specific, and you know the keywords that your potential client uses, it is very easy to position yourself in the first position. I have done it with many words and in very competitive markets. You just have to know what you do, nothing more. You might be thinking, what am I getting out of all this? Yes, we have discussed the business benefits, but once again, I feel the need to do a quick and detailed reminder of why videos are a really attractive format.

It is not the same to arrive at a website where there are only words and more words than when we see the odd video between the paragraphs.

The user experience is much more intense, more fun, and relaxed. People seek comfort and enjoyment with what we do, so the more you make them enjoy, the better. You will always achieve better results in Google searches.

As I already indicated, YouTube belongs to Google, so they are a united platform. Increasingly. What does that mean? The objective of Google is to offer the most relevant results when a person searches for something in their search engine.

If Google detects that your video has many visits, there are many links to it; then, it is worth a recommendation. The good thing about this is that it will appear in the search with the first frame of the video next to the link. A very attractive way to get results and with which you will get all the clicks. I assure you.

Remember, whether you like it or not, Google is King. I recommend that you join him for the benefit of your business. Take advantage of their tools. Creating videos is a lot of fun as well. Although at first, you are afraid or embarrassed to make videos where your face comes out, it is normal. It happens to all of us.

We are not used to seeing each other. We all are listening to the voices in our heads. Looking at your face in the mirror feels dreadful. When you hear or see yourself in a video, it's a feeling of "depersonalization." Getting used to it will take a few months but neglect that in the end, you will end up accepting yourself as you are. Do not hesitate.

Once you have overcome the barrier that separates your image from your mind, the rest will be sewing and singing. Also, you will have a great time making these videos. They take time; I have to tell you that too. Remember! We all reject our voice and image when we see each other on video. Learn to accept that this is you. Don't be afraid of "not liking" a video.

Even with all the current advancements in digital technology, how do you know, as a creator, if you're reaching the same audience? Are you reaching the same target audience that you want to reach from one fenced garden to another? Much attention has been paid to the accuracy of data in identifying the correct audience during planning, but what about identifying the audience in various media?

If data and audience discovery and modeling were the brains of a campaign, audience activation should be the heart. In the early days of digital advertising, cookies identified audiences, helped learn their digital behaviors, add more data, and activate them by synchronizing cookies. However, with devices being common and with the rise of social media, the complexity of buying prints for a customer from one medium to another requires more than just data and technology.

The ability to connect individually with your audience across all touchpoints without sacrificing the accuracy and integrity of your audience definition should be the very foundation on which all media purchases rest. It is the promise of reaching audiences beyond limits. And that promise could come true if we use digital thinking and use the tools at our disposal.

The current process is the current problem. Today, the typical imprecise customer segmentation process works like this: creating segments based on so-called "identities." For example, Harry, an active man between 18 and 34 years of age; Martha, a mother who lives in a residential neighborhood and has school-age children, or Tony, an outdoor enthusiast on the weekends. The problem is that this segment represents an imaginary goal that doesn't exist. When those "identities" are reached, there is no assurance that they are open to viewing your content. Even if you reach a potential pool of audience, there is no way to determine if they have had the optimal level of exposure across a platform.

In a nutshell: in the traditional system, a lot of money is wasted in the media, and people who could be activated are not reached. Avoid carpet-bombing. The segmentation process should start with universal identifiers associated with real people doing real things on various media and devices.

Now we know that video is one of the main attractions for content marketing today. The trend is growing and points to that during the next year, where YouTube marketing will be one of the main bets for digital *media* campaigns.

In YouTube marketing, there are two golden rules for the objectives that you set for yourself: progressively increase the volume of content and only offer quality content that maintains engagement with your audience. The symbiosis of these two golden rules will be the basis of success in implementing your YouTube marketing strategy.

So, you ask: what objectives are pursued with YouTube marketing? Do I need to go back to school and get a degree? No. It's quite simple. Increasing the volume of publications creates expectations in the audience. It is a good *teaser* to take the first steps in your YouTube marketing strategy.

After the generation of interest, the most important thing will be to maintain regularity in the days that you make publications. This way, you will be able to create a routine of visits to your audience. Educate the audience to visit your channel (daily, weekly, etc.).

The holy grail of reaching your target audience
Once you start making videos, investigate, and observe your environment. As in any other strategy, the first step should be to observe your competition and see what it offers to its customers. Discover what the keys to its success are. See how it delivers the offer and what are the main strengths. You should look at what your competition does on its channels and how it

does it.

The objective of this market analysis is to find out what your competitive advantage could be that will lead you to differentiate yourself from the rest and position you as a leading brand in a certain market niche. It is very important to do this first step carefully before launching content for users.

Content Bucket list

Once you have researched and observed the environment, you can move on to creating content lists. Create a 'Content Bucket' list and stick to it. It is about designing the 'master lines' in which the content of your channel will move. It is very important to offer valuable content, and the best way to do it is by designing a strategy based on content buckets.

For example: Suppose your channel reviews tech products, and your goal is to reach more subscribers, build your credibility, and smile next to Unbox Therapy and iJustine. To gain more views, the content will be directed to different 'content cubes' as tutorials that highlight the benefits and use of certain devices.

Your content is aimed at seeing the different possibilities and innovations that the products you review have.

Set the rules and educate your audience

Your channel should follow a broadcast routine. Once the tone and the different content buckets or themes adapted to the videos, it will be time to establish broadcasting terms. How often are you going to offer the content? What day and time is it better to offer a certain type of content? In which social networks are you going to boost YouTube videos?

It's about setting the frequency and establishing routines that help educate the audience in the right direction, generating a desire and a habit of visiting your channel. Respecting the frequency of publication is essential to generate interest and not deceive users.

For example, if you upload an explanatory video with the news for the week every Monday and Friday, you publish a summary video with the content of the week.

It is highly recommended that you do not change this routine from one day to the next. In the case of changing the frequency of publications, it must be for a justified reason. Make it clear to your followers and users what the new publication period will be to maintain that routine of visits to your YouTube channel.

Make it clear what the dynamics of the channel will be. Apart from that, the days of publication, themes, and always invite people to share the video and make comments. These comments will emerge the possible changes and new directions that you will take for future videos.

Add subtitles to your videos

If you want to improve the user experience, you must add subtitles to your videos. Most people watch videos from their smartphone or tablet and often do so with low sound, no sound, or in public with background noise.

And of course, if the user does not know what is said in the video, he will go to the next video and will not see it. Let's not forget the differently-abled people. It's 2020, and inclusivity matters. A trick: take advantage of the subtitle texts to create a post on a blog.

Also, you will prevent others from extracting that text content and taking advantage of it (yes, it happens very often).

Pitching your videos to a larger audience

One strategy is collaboration. It is the basis of success on a platform like YouTube. The biggest YouTubers and successful brands use collaboration in their YouTube marketing campaigns. In the digital world, it is not a barrier for the brand but quite the opposite. It's a win-win. Thinking contrary to this can hurt your channel or brand. We will talk about collaboration later. Right now, we will explore how your channel can target videos to a larger audience. All you have to do is indicate the YouTube algorithm about your audience.

For this, you must make a good selection of keywords both in the title, in the description, and the tags. Know appropriate keywords for the target audience to which you want to direct your video. The keywords of your niche are common words. You can expand that number of keywords by researching tools that will provide other keywords that are also searched by the users you want to target. For this research, we will use two tools, one from Google and the other from YouTube. With Google AdWords, an external tool helps us find the number of searches a specific keyword has. If we see that it has a good number of searches, we can add it as a keyword in our dictionary. The YouTube keyword tool will provide us with the most popular words on YouTube.

They will also be added to our keyword collection. Both tools are studied in a previous post as tools for choosing keywords on YouTube. You also have other tools provided by Google to find future trends in keywords of your sector or niche. Google Trends will indicate the results of searches carried out for the keywords you give it to study over the past years. It will mark you a trend line for future dates.

You can see a study on trends and how you can take advantage of it. With this research, you compose a video title. This action can be performed while a video is being uploaded to your YouTube channel. In the description, try adding a compound phrase formed with the keywords of your niche.

The articles and prepositions are not important. They do not position. They help to form the phrase, but they are not picked up by the YouTube algorithm. You can add a URL to your website. With this link, the users to whom the video appears can visit it.

If you are a YouTube partner, you can add this URL on the same video playback screen as a link to the associated website. You can go to the main page or a specific page within that associated URL.

The description must include the appropriate keywords separated by commas. The more we add, the better we can write simple words or words made up of two or three but with a limit of up to 15.

Similar words will appear under the label drawer. You can add them but only the ones closest to your niche.

Facebook it, Instagram it, Twitter it, Snapchat it, don't LinkedIn it

It's a rule of thumb. You must have an active profile associated with your YouTube channel. The profile pictures must also be the same, and there must not be anything distinctive in the page titles. Share it across your social media platforms during appropriate times.

Search which time is appropriate for posting content. If you are just getting started, this may be irrelevant to you. Beginners should keep pace with posting on all networks. You can get closer to your target audience.

If the content is great, and they seem to relate to it, it will surely circulate. The first moments after uploading the video are important because that's when you see how users interact. If in that period, not many sharing actions are carried out, they are not very interested. But this does not mean your video is forgotten. The video stays.

Over time the interest may change and be searched on any other occasion. In any case, the links marked within the video and in the description serve as YouTube links that point to your website. If you optimize your website with Google's Webmaster Tools, you can see that

YouTube links are marked as inbound.

However, they do not transfer to the YouTube PageRank stream because they are no-follow links. The search engine algorithms do not follow them. If your video is embedded on another website or blog, it goes to that YouTube video, giving it relevance.

Reaching viewers in your neighborhood and Norway

Rome was not built in a day or even weeks for that matter. The same goes for growing a channel and building a strong fanbase. Imagine the pool of competitors waiting to cash in opportunities and having the same desire for success.

Everyone can Google and find unique ways to promote their channel. So, where do you draw the line and stand out? The key is to create unmatchable content. Got a favorite YouTuber? What do you like most about them?

Quality content is the game changer. Strive to establish yourself as the ideal expert in your domain and make your channel a valuable resource for people. Most popular YouTubers do the same. Walk in the shoes of your subscribers. What are the challenges? Got any questions? What ticks them? Most importantly, understand what they need. That is why you must always check the metrics of your YouTube channel and proceed with it.

Not only does it reveal facts about your audience but will also help with creating engaging content. In this way, you can give them value, which will be paid through engagement: views, likes, comments, and ultimately, subscriptions.

Ask yourself before making a video: "What value will it bring to my audience?" Continue the process of creating your video once you have the answer.

Create irresistible videos on your YouTube channel: keep it precise yet informative; plan a story arc beforehandand follow a script;cover specific topics and try to elicit audience engagement; incorporate custom captions to your videos; dive into software for video editing; and if you cannot create a slideshow, animation or a presentation, you canavail free or paid templates available on the web.

Not everything works for everyone. The job is to find out what makes your viewers stick around and not quit.

Focus on the content creation process, and come up with realistic goals and topics you want to consider, analyze your audience's and provide content accordingly. What you want is to promote your videos on YouTube, right?

Therefore, create a platform for your viewers, a place they will never want to leave voluntarily. Besides, do not leave an empty profile. Some YouTubers rush straight into creating content. They simply don't bother filling out their account profile. However, an attractive profile is an effective way to promote your channel. There are several practices to complete your profile. Start by adhering to a consistent writing style, design, and color palette that matches your other channels, social media, and website. This will help viewers identify your brand more easily and differentiate yours from a billion other channels.

When creating a description, you should include keywords without abusing too many penalties incurred for excessive use of keywords. It's also ideal for posting content on a set schedule. With this, you will train the audience of that predefined calendar. This should make your users always search for more content on your channel.

It will also help provide a measure of the consistency that users love. Share in your mailing list. If you are already incorporating email marketing strategies, do not miss this option. And if you don't, you don't know the opportunities you're missing!

So, when you design your next newsletter, include a reference to the latest videos you have uploaded to YouTube. Those who receive emails are already interested in your content. So surely, they will also be interested in watching your videos.

"I live with my parents and don't have to pay rent. How can I invest in promoting my videos?"

The truth about promoting your YouTube videos through ads

If you are interested in setting aside a budget to promote, I don't mind. Google Ads is a proven option. It remains a popular and effective advertising model on the Internet. And it is ideal for advertising your video campaigns.

Advertising on this platform is very diverse. It lets you create different types of ads, depending on what your main objectives are. YouTube offers different options and very detailed segmentation. It allows you to reach many potential customers with precise segmentation. You can decide how much money you want to spend on this type of promotion.

The possibilities that Google AdWords offers to advertise a YouTube video are different. Some of them are:

Ads in stream

They are included in other videos and can be skipped once the user has viewed the first five seconds. I'm sure you know exactly what ads I'm talking about. These campaigns can be played during or after a video. For this type of campaign, only the CPV (Cost Per View) bid is enabled. AdWords will charge you nothing if a viewer skips the ad after viewing a minimum of five seconds, and the playtime does not cover at least 30 seconds. Conversely, if the user gets to see the entire ad or close to 30 seconds, AdWords will charge it based on your CPV bid.

To create such a campaign, you must follow certain steps: The first is to select the video you want to display. Create the text carrying information about you or your channel, which includes a title and a description. You will also be asked to select a thumbnail image, which will be the first thing users do before clicking on the ad.

Choose where you want to redirect the users when they click on the ad. Add the URL of a web page or your own YouTube channel so that they see more content. You can absolutely parameterize a daily budget. You can modify it.

You have two ways to select the target audience: People who search the YouTube app itself or people who are viewing a video.

TrueView Video Discovery

These ads appear in the list of results when a user performs a search. They may also appear in the list of related videos shown on the right margin while the user is viewing a video. These types of campaigns also have the only way to select the CPV bidding system.

To create this campaign, follow the same steps as in the case of in-stream campaigns. Both are created in the TrueView "video" campaign type. Simply select one type or another at the beginning of the campaign creation.

Bumper Ads

Bumper Ads do not exceed six seconds in length displayed while the user is watching a video. Being so short, the viewer cannot skip it. To create this type of ad, you must: Create a new video campaign. Define the objectives of the subtype. Assign it a name. Establish the budget you will have and the maximum CPM (Cost per 1000 Impressions). Once the ad is selected, specify that the video type is Bumper Ad. Go ahead and try it for yourself. The creation of YouTube campaigns is a great option to make yourself known, given the great popularity that the video platform has achieved. Don't think about it anymore. Jump in.

AdWords allows you to place and manage video ads through the Google Display Network. Its wide coverage means that it can reach practically anywhere in the world, reaching its audience wherever it is. When Google bought YouTube in 2006, in addition to buying the most important online video portal, it accessed an audience of 800 million people every month.

Together with its already wide and powerful Display Network, it makes AdWords one of the best tools to manage video campaigns, obtaining measurable and quantifiable results from the performance of your ads. You can track the scope of the tour campaign: Your ads will appear on the most important online video website.

More than 800 million people visit YouTube a month, and hundreds of millions of hours of video are watched every day. The Display Network is a big deal: In addition to YouTube's own formats, your videos can also be published on the Google Display Network. This network currently comprises more than 2 million websites on different topics. AdWords means accurate segmentation.

Google AdWords for video allows precise segmentation by selecting different options: keywords, demographics, location, topics, category of interests, etc. Pay Per Video display (CPV) is cost-effective: Video ads that you can configure with AdWords belong to the TrueView family, which means that you will only pay when the user decides to watch your video.

This gives you the security that you are only paying for the ads that the user has viewed in full. You have the insights: Thanks to analytics, you will obtain valuable information (who watches the video, how long, demographics) that will be used to optimize campaign performance and improve ads.

I advise you so that your investment in YouTube advertising is highly profitable, and you get the best results. It is vital to choose the ideal YouTube advertising format for the type of potential customers and the achievement of the objectives set with the campaign, within the different models offered by YouTube.

That is why we use our knowledge and experience in YouTube AdWords to advise you on whether it is convenient for you to advertise in-stream or in search format or slate format.

Publish press releases

If you are thinking about massively reaching the public, this one's for you. This mechanism will take longer, but they are also interesting, and it all adds up. Create press releases, mention the video, your channel, and publish on specialized news agencies in your niche.

You can also pitch blogs and websites related to your niche, which you have previously contacted at a cold door or certain events. They seemed to have shown interest in receiving press releases about your platform.

"Yes, I want to be talking about Huda Beauty or the Cybertruck in my videos."

Branded content: an extension to engaging your target audience

YouTube content creators have communities of millions of content-hungry users. These are exciting possibilities. But the days of representational videos where you smile and promote a product are long gone.

If done well, collaborations on YouTube can be much more playful. It's very simple: brands HAVE messages, YouTubers put the style and energy, and viewers consume the content. Although it is not that easy.

When a creator shares the limelight with a brand, the content must be authentic, be suitable for its exclusive audience, and, at the same time, integrate a brand story. Success needs a common purpose, creative potential, and a healthy dose of subtlety. Recently, YouTube invited experts to talk about what has and has not worked during this first-generation of YouTube collaborations. This book carries information from the experts who attended and summarized into key points for creators themselves. The concept of "fame" is changing. YouTube content creators are recognized for who they are in real life rather than playing characters in frames.

So, it's no surprise that Tom Punch, VICE Media's CEO and Global Creative, claims that in all content collaborations that have been put to him, the word "authenticity" is specifically mentioned in the proposal.

Authenticity is an easy concept that everyone talks about. It is astonishingly simple but woefully infrequent. What does it mean? How is it demonstrated? In the case of YouTube collaborations, let's agree that authenticity is reached by respecting a brand's values and by affiliating with a creator who shares a common purpose.

Shabnam Mogharabi, the creator of SoulPancake, is dedicated to publishing inspiring content, which has garnered over 200 million views in less than three years. She stressed that collaborations have to be authentic to the audience. If your audience doesn't expect certain content from your channel, then don't publish it. If it's not meaningful, your subscribers will not share it. *That is a Bible verse right there.*

Purina Tidy Cats collaborated with SoulPancake to engage with Generation Y cat owners. They established the most important values shared by both brands: optimism, a stress-free life, and love for kittens. They then created a video which hit over eight million views. Can you imagine that? So, the key is not to just post but create, as goes the term "content creator."

The autonomy of YouTubers is based not only on offering content that many people see, but on creating communities. Take Hannah Hart. She sits on two million subscribers with the weekly video series "My Drunk Kitchen."

She maintains constant engagement with her subscribers and even considers them boardroom members since they suggest recipes and are not afraid to express their opinions when they like something. *We need that level of seriousness.*

This level of synergy can be novel for a brand, so it is important to understand what discussions are already taking place. How can a brand participate in these constant conversations without interrupting them? Pam Scheideler, Executive Vice President and Director of Digital Production at Deutsch LA, views that brands should not consider YouTubers as distribution channels and tell them what to say about their product or service.

Appearing suddenly and endorsing regardless of audience reaction, is the easiest way to end the conversation and an absolute no-brainer. Pam highlighted an example of a collaboration in which there was a genuine relationship between the brand and the YouTuber. But for the followers, this was suspicious because they did not receive what they expected.

Pam's company collaborated with Pizza Hut for a natural collaboration with 'Jack and Jack'. They were seen making pizzas in the Pizza Hut test kitchen. What everyone missed is what was 'Jack and Jack' offering to their audience.

Followers were accustomed to watching new music or humor videos on their channel. Yet they had offered them a video in which 'Jack and Jack' cooked and ate pizza. Followers quickly demonstrated their discontent in the comments.

You also have to loosen the reins a bit. Advertising agencies learn from how YouTubers approach their audience and what drives them to come back for more. Nick Barham, Strategic Director of TBWA, thinks that more and more influencers create content without a specific narrative and a clear message.

This may be a risky route for brands. However, if we disregard the need to create something carried in the beginning, in the middle and at the end, we can open ourselves to more possibilities.

I think the interesting thing about collaborating with YouTubers is that they are contributing video content on their platform, and they think very differently about storytelling. Matt Johnson, director of Group Strategy at 72andSunny, thinks that agencies can forget about part of that exclusivity that revolves around the creative process.

It would mean not focusing on production value but allowing the YouTubers to be themselves rather than imagining them to unquestionably submit to the brand's demands. No one's a robot or a slave here.

Matt believes that in the end, if you loosen the reins and forget about the exclusivity that revolves around the standard creative process, you will create something more effective – not just another ad-based video that your users frown upon.

72andSunny's hit "Left Swipe Dat" did the same. A few YouTube celebrities made their original contribution in a video and once published, fans were asked to share videos by playback of the song.

By including the audience in the creative crunch, some control had to be put aside in the process, but this allowed the conversation to stay engaged even after the original video was released.

So innovative. Moving on, ask yourself: who's even going to like this? YouTube allows users to choose from billions of videos, but by giving more options, more filters need to be added.

Users will not interact with the content if they simply agree or disagree with it. Tom shares that VICE has a whole network of digital channels centered on cultural subjects and alternative stories. Perhaps that is why some of VICE's most popular videos may be rated "somewhat weird" by the majority of people.

Nonetheless, he believes that the next generation's branding will cover those subcultures, that alternative facet, and not so much popular culture and famous people as always. Hint: Middle East. Recent studies have shown that some YouTube celebrities are more influential and popular than typical celebrities among young Americans.

This means that creators must answer a million-dollar question: who is going to love this? Stuart Smith from Anomaly says that creators should ask themselves from the beginning: "Will the audience share it?" If brands and creators do not create content with these issues in mind, it will be forgotten.

It is a fantastic opportunity for brands. What cultural spectrum do you want to cover? What kind of content can you create to inspire people to become even more immersed in their interests? To reach that Gen Y audience, brands should maintain some freshness and tell avant-garde stories. This is a very different approach to marketing. It is not about seeking the attention of the masses, but it can generate a community that is involved and engaged.

III

YouTube algorithm: how not to turn it into a nightmare

If you want to be a successful YouTuber, it is logical that you understand the YouTube algorithm and how it works. Let me tell you: YouTube Algorithm is the one you need to befriend first. Getting everything according to how the algorithm is challenging for even the biggest YouTubers out there.

I don't wish to suggest that it is a bottleneck but it is one aspect that may haunt you in your entire YouTube journey if you're getting it wrong. It is the hinge. It is the very pivot everything stands on. To your surprise, it never remains the same.

YouTube is committed to offering a rewarding broadcasting experience, and it uses algorithms to make it possible. YouTube is King Henry VIII, and the algorithm is Thomas Cromwell. You have come to the right place because this book carries everything you want to know about the algorithm before you start making some serious money.

All or most of your questions will be answered satisfactorily. The YouTube algorithm is a recommendation system for users of the platform. Engineers describe it as "one of the complex and most sophisticated industrial recommendation systems in existence today."

This way, we can answer the question, "what in the world is the YouTube algorithm?" in the following way: it is a system controlled by artificial intelligence that oversees ordering, profiling, and recommending videos to users using their history and their interaction on the platform.

You may be wondering how it affects you. Well, it affects you a lot. What happens is that no one notices unless they start experiencing irregularities and wonder how this works or why it works this way. YouTubers tend to have the biggest problems when it comes to algorithms within YouTube.

Above all, novice creators, those who are starting, can face a multitude of challenges. But you don't have to worry. You don't have to be the most experienced YouTuber out there either.

This impressive system that uses artificial intelligence to manage a database with hundreds of millions of videos and billions of users has two main objectives: help viewers find videos with the content they want to watch which enables maximize engagement and long-term viewer satisfaction. Also, to get users to spend more time on a channel and make more profit from the advertisements.

Like most Artificial Intelligence resources, YouTube's AI is surprisingly advanced and sophisticated. YouTube has published only small and insignificant pieces of information related to its system. They published a book in 2016 called "Deep Neural Networks for YouTube Recommendations."

This book clarifies some small details, and people have managed to obtain a little more information from the company's ex-employees. But despite this, the information remains very secret. If you are interested in YouTube, you will also want to manage numbers.

To understand how the YouTube algorithm works, we must go a bit on the subject and talk about the surface, since it is a somewhat complex and profound subject. We know its main function is to serve as a recommendation system for users, to offer a unique service that makes you want to quit your job and spend every afternoon watching videos while making money with advertising. But recommending videos on a platform that moves such an amount of information per second is extremely challenging. We can understand it from different perspectives: most recommendation algorithms that exist today are proven to work optimally with small issues; they don't work on a scale as huge as YouTube's.

These are highly specialized learning algorithms that can distribute tasks and are required to offer an efficient service and correct information management every time they are deployed. YouTube has a very dynamic corpus.

With each passing second, many hours of video are uploaded to the servers. So, the recommendation system must analyze and model the newly loaded content. At the same time, it must consider the actions taken by billions of users worldwide. It is inherently difficult to predict a user's behavior despite having their historical behavior stored on YouTube.

It is due to scarcity and a variety of unobservable external factors. It's almost impossible for YouTube's algorithm to get the fundamental truth about user satisfaction. This complicates modeling, understanding it, and generates noise in the information. A big load of mess. You can find neural networks and advanced programming in the YouTube algorithm.

The YouTube algorithm or the recommendation system is made up of two neural networks: the first, for the "generation of candidates"; the second, for "the ranking." At this point, you may feel like being on a tour of Elon Musk's The Boring Company.

Let me break down this information. The neural network is in charge of "generating channels." It picks elements from the user's activity history on the platform as input and retrieves a small subset of hundreds of videos from the large YouTube corpus. These channels are generally relevant to the user.

This is why you get recommended similar artists and songs released every time you play that Cardi B song. With powerful precision, this network, through collaborative filtering, provides extensive customization.

The neural network that works with "the ranking" performs its task assigning scores to each video with a single objective and using a rich set of characteristics that describe the video and the user.

As a result, those videos with the highest scores are presented to the user. This two-stage recommendation system allows them to make recommendations on an extremely large corpus (hundreds of millions of videos). In this way, they ensure that the moderate number of videos that appear for the user on the screen are personalized and attractive.

It is important to say that for the development of such a process, the YouTube algorithm makes extensive use of offline metrics (precision, recovery, loss of classification, among others) to continue producing improvements to the system.

"Can I tweak the algorithm?"

How to change the algorithm of YouTube? Can we change the Facebook algorithm? Could we change the Google algorithm? The answer is No. Impossible. Nobody can change the YouTube algorithm unless you are the engineer in charge of the system in the company itself.

Furthermore, according to YouTube spokespersons, the algorithm keeps changing, evolving, and learning from users and their interactions; all thanks to artificial intelligence. So, the latest changes on YouTube are due to this reason. We can understand that the YouTube 2018 algorithm and the YouTube 2019 algorithm have already been or are about to become obsolete.

How not to mess with it?

Entering or being picked by the YouTube algorithm is extremely important if you want the videos you upload to your channel to be seen numerous times and, even more, if you want to receive income for it. I will give you a heads up to enter the YouTube algorithm and to succeed in its recommendations.

First, the algorithm favors a consistent format. All major YouTube channels or series can summarize much of their success in two words, consistency and coherence. Consistency is the most important pillar of success on YouTube, and consistency keeps them stable and growing. It keeps the algorithm happy.

Without them, it is possible to capture the attention of viewers and they will not be able to be preserved over time. This can be seen in many YouTube channels in which people try to gain as much attention as possible. They treat their channel as a place where they can dump content, rather than as a temple of videos.

YouTube channels that are capable of sustainably increasing their number of subscribers and viewers is because they have found consistency. Consistency makes it much easier for people to decide to watch more of the same content and subscribe to the channel.

Channels such as Nas Daily, with 1.1 million subscribers, is a clear and successful example that consistency in the content they offer is part of the key: a minute or two long videos on travel adventures, cultures, and political subjects with simplest explanations.

Maintaining consistency, along with good material, will lead to a growth in the number of subscribers in the medium or long term. If you're lucky enough to have one of the channel's videos go viral for a while, it's the best chance for some of those viewers (who only came in for the particular video) to become long-term subscribers.

This will happen if those viewers find more of the same or similar videos on the channel if they find consistency. You can also boost the recommendation engine from various sources. Not surprisingly, the newest channels on YouTube can't expect the referral engine to generate all or most of their views, because no one knows them.

They have almost no reproductions, and the algorithm does not have much information that relates them to what users are looking for. That is because recommendations are primarily based on interaction of viewers and their YouTube history.

Remember that YouTube's algorithm is about thousands of code lines that are responsible for collecting the data generated by users in the channels to give future and personalized recommendations.

So being new, we must find other means that stimulate the growth of our channel so that, in the future, it will be the algorithm that does the work of coming to light.

We must get down to work and practice all the usual means with which it is possible to promote our videos for the algorithm to catch it. Send the latest videos to an email list. Search for advertising through blogs, influencers, or other YouTubers.

Promote yourself through social networks. Do not miss any of the important ones: Twitter, Facebook, Instagram, TikTok, and any other in which you have people who read, listen, or see you. SEO on YouTube – yes, we will come to that later. It is one of the most important and relevant ways from any point of view.

With the right keywords in the title and the description of the video, you can gain ground to the algorithm and manage to appear among the first options, even when your channel is almost unknown. Obtaining more subscribers is one of the best ways that can ensure you keep a rhythm of views in your videos that could make you relevant to the algorithm and be recommended by it. The algorithm supports thumbnail images. This is a point of great importance. Thumbnails can be a magnet for viewers to click your video and enter, or they can simply be ignored as they are not curious about the video title or thumbnail. The algorithm is programmed to recommend videos with catchy and relevant thumbnails.

It also recommends videos with faces in thumbnails. If we see among the popular YouTube videos, we will quickly notice that there are many expressive faces among the video thumbnails. They long understood the work of algorithms in promoting such videos.

To get more clicks that give us views and relevance to the YouTube algorithm, we must have very striking thumbnails. Tattoo that on your skin.

What is recommended are close-ups of emotional faces or shots of moments of action. Understand that emotions are an efficient way to convey complex nuances. It is popular knowledge that humans are programmed to respond to faces.

We have seen that this is consistent across all media. But it is important to note that faces with complex emotions outweigh stoic or benign expressions.

Another important trend, according to algorithms, is that a thumbnail image that contains more than three people is less likely to beat those who only had three or less. From what emerged, the so-called rule or guide of thirdsis ideal for composing thumbnails.

This suggests us placing the point of interest in the first or last third of the painting and promises to make the images have an ideal proportion so that the brains process them faster and attract the viewer's attention to the message.

Texts on thumbnails are another point of great relevance to algorithms. Why? According to YouTube, the thumbnail concerning the title almost guarantees to cause the viewer's eyes to focus on the video thumbnail first. And, if the image seems attractive enough, they will read the title. You can try that now.

There is also one more way to take advantage of your miniatures, similarly personalizing them in each video and making them your channel brand. In this way, your subscribers will find you more easily, and you will maintain much more consistency. As I said, the algorithm is the most sophisticated recommendation.

You must also invite and encourage viewers to stay after entering the video. Getting people to enter our videos is one thing. Making them watch a video to the end is another, very different, and complicated but not possible.

The algorithm wants you to do exactly that. You can improve the completion rates in your videos and gain more playing time. Start your videos with energy and spreading good spirits. It incorporates a hook in the introduction of the video: striking information, creating a doubt, generating expectations.

Analyze the average amount of time to where viewers go and stop watching the video, so you can adjust the next ones. Transcribe the videos in your native language (later and if your subscribers suggest it, add more languages), so that they can be viewed without volume and by more people.

At this point, the algorithm is smiling at you. Use the jump cuts in the video and the exchange of shots to avoid that these can bore the viewer. If the video is long, encourage it, bring it to life, change the setting, and whatever it takes to keep the user entertained, wanting to see the full clip and perhaps go for another video on the channel.

Moreover, encourage and promote activity on your channel. You may think I am bluffing, but I bet you this is how the algorithm works. A good activity on your channel is synonymous with success.

Some of the ways that can make it easier for viewers to decide to see more of your content is using end cards to manually recommend related videos from your channel. Prepare playlists that link your videos and thus ensure that at the end of the video, the next one is always yours. As I mentioned, create a channel with a coherent and consistent format - from the thumbnail image of the videos to their content.

In this way, if viewers enjoy one of our clips, they will reasonably assume that the others will also be to their liking, and the algorithm will do its magic. Add scenes from other videos to induce viewers to consume more content. Make calls to action and interact with those who comment on our videos.

YouTube algorithm is programmed to ensure monetization

YouTube's algorithm has been changing over the years, but one thing remains the same, and its objective is to make more people see and participate in more videos on the platform. My recommendations will help you to get more clicks and relevance on the YouTube algorithm. Your channel's videos will be more recommended to the platform's user community.

YouTube works as a social network but is focused solely on videos, regardless of their length. It stores almost any type of videos that users upload (that comply with company policies), in the most modern formats. YouTube's operation focuses on its business model and evolves in favor of its growth, the sale of advertising.

These are sometimes-annoying ads that interrupt videos we are playing and make us wait five seconds to skip. The company offers brands, companies, or individuals the opportunity to advertise their products or services through user channels that meet certain requirements; Minimum of 4,000 hours of playback per year and 1,000 subscribers.

YouTube charges those who want advertising, it keeps one part, and the other is for the YouTuber. The remunerations for content creators are quite good, and they are so because they are the soul of YouTube.

Without them, the company would not make sense. To increase the hours that users spend on YouTube and, in the same way, the profits. This is how the mysterious algorithm comes into action.

For everyone, and regardless of why we enter the page or the application, the operation of YouTube is quite simple. It does not require great knowledge or skills to take advantage of all its possibilities.

However, from that point until the moment that your videos are played thousands or millions of times, or that you can collect a royalty, it is far and requires a lot of effort. Viewers are just looking for fun, information, or entertainment.

How the algorithm works for them is much, much easier. And, to the point that they do not need

43

to have a YouTube account for it. But it is always easier to find the videos they are interested in if they have a registered user. It will be convenient for them to subscribe to the channels of YouTube that create the content they like.

They will have recommendations for related videos, which is surely an opportunity for you.

"I want to beat the algorithm. Bring on the octagon"

About the YouTube algorithm, there is a lot of secrecy regarding its specific operation and the codes that make it up. The idea of modifying or beating it for that matter is quite absurd unless you are not an engineer working within the company.

However, not being able to modify it does not mean not being able to understand it or being able to take advantage of it. Although, of course, it has a certain complexity, as you have already read in the pages above. It is simply about creating a YouTube channel that is coherent and consistent in content and audience, with attractive and well-structured videos.

Use SEO to achieve positioning and then be recommended. We will come to SEO shortly. In short, we cannot beat the YouTube algorithm like in other times. We can only join it and find the best ways for our content to be recommended by it.

I guarantee that you can do it if you follow the advice I have already given you.

The updated algorithm

As time went by, many wondered what the YouTube algorithm is. It has created a somewhat negative vision among the viewers, YouTubers, and advertisers of the platform. This is something that the company is aware of. Of course, it is vital to know how the current algorithm works.

Currently, the algorithm's artificial intelligence focuses on a recommendation system built from videos that match user preferences. Just like in the old days. It includes special characteristics to later reorder the list based on the information stored in history. It also takes into account the clicks used, the likes given, and other interactions.

They are all variables that, when placed in the algorithm formulas, form an inventory for future recommendations. Despite the sophistication, YouTube has had controversies worldwide for cases of invasion of privacy, pedophilia, and even alteration of trends in presidential elections, among many more.

A group of responsible researchers and engineers within the company recently published a study called: "Recommendations about which video to watch next: a multitasking classification system." We can also expect possible improvements to the YouTube algorithm. In this way, the company proposes a possible solution to the problems that plague the company, an update of the YouTube base algorithm.

The latest update recommends even more specific content to users to achieve a more sophisticated level of detail in the recommendation process. While they intend to retain the same operating principle of the algorithm, they want to use every effort to avoid "implicit bias," a term they use and refers to the influence of recommendations on user behavior.

According to the study, the results reveal that implicit bias complicates the task of knowing if the user clicked on a video because it "looks recommendable" or because they liked it. Over time, it generates an effect that ends up distancing the viewer more and more from the videos that s/he wanted to see or would be useful to him/her.

To prevent this bias from continuing to negatively impact users, the engineers propose that the position of the video in the recommendation sidebar the viewer clicks be evaluated. Using this data as the primary source of information will make the other videos that were shown as the first option lose weight and relevance among the recommendations.

They seek to limit the contagion effect generated by the experience of other users. A way to achieve a consistent and more personalized experience for each user or visitor. It is obvious that there have been many changes and that these have been necessary and implemented in YouTube's search and recommendation algorithms on YouTube over time.

It is part of the evolution of the largest and most important video social network on the planet, one with more than one and a half billion active users monthly. From its founding until 2012, YouTube rated its videos by view counts, by their popularity.

The more viewers watched a video, liked it, and shared it, the more frequently it would be presented to other viewers. At first, everything was going well for the company and the first YouTubers. However, the downside was that people soon understood how the system worked and learned to manipulate the algorithm easily.

The manipulation of the YouTube algorithm

Simple! The only thing they had to do was put "click baits" on the titles of their videos to attract viewers and enter them, making them see a small part of the content. And of course, everyone quickly realized that the video was not about what the title promised and stopped watching it. Countless clickbait video complaints echoed so much that YouTube had to change in 2012 and, for the first time, its algorithm significantly. This time prioritizing the length (video viewing time) and session count (total time dedicated).

Again, and in a short time, YouTubers understood and learned that the best way to beat the algorithm was to create long-lasting videos and thus be able to fulfill the basic premise.

The difference on that occasion was that the solution turned out to be very exhausting for content creators; they started to run out. It was not at all easy to keep creating long videos. They required huge amounts of new, fresh, and attractive content for viewers.

YouTubers had to keep creating the same number of videos as ever, but with more time to cover and fewer resources. A moment that some knew how to take advantage of successfully, managing to amass millions of followers.

PewDiePie is an example of how to manipulate YouTube. This was the case of the YouTuber who, today, has more than 100 million subscribers on his channel, PewDiePie. Long-duration videos for him were no problem since he was recorded playing video games for hours.

A strategy that was incredibly effective compared to videos that normally require prior planning for their production, script, and material resources. Implementation of Artificial Intelligence (AI) also happened.

In 2016, intending to stay as the social network and the leading video storage and distribution platform, YouTube implemented artificial intelligence and machine learning to its search and recommendation algorithm.

That greatly altered the behavior and material of the YouTubers who wanted to stay in the place they had come to and that of those who aspired to have a career. This is because the recommendations that came to the viewers were different; conspiracy theories and false news stood out.

The 2016 United States Presidential Election is an example of the power of the YouTube algorithm. One of the most notorious cases for the strange videos promoted by the algorithm's artificial intelligence was during the presidential elections in the United States. According to the

British newspaper The Guardian, the Republican candidate Donald Trump was given more than 86% of the recommendations on YouTube, making him more and more popular.

On the other hand, for Hillary Clinton, the story was another, a different and negative one. During the time of the elections, the most recommended channel was Alex Jones, one on conspiracy theoristswho distanced the country from reality. Of course, he also spoke ill of Hillary Clinton.

Other channels highly recommended by the algorithm discredited the candidate in any way (health problems, sexual orientation, and many pointless accusations) or spoke highly of Donald Trump. YouTube representatives gave their version: "Our search and referral system reflect what people are looking for, the number of videos available, and the videos people most choose to watch on YouTube. There are no inclinations towards any candidate; it is the reflection of the spectator's interest."

Take Guillaume Chaslot, former Google and co-developer of the algorithm, who has a doctorate in Artificial Intelligence and a key engineer behind YouTube algorithm. He was disappointed after his three years staying over the project and told The Guardian: "YouTube is something that looks like reality, but it is distorted so that you spend more time online. The recommendation algorithm is not optimizing what is true, balanced, or healthy for democracies."

The AI doctor added that the algorithm constantly keeps changing and learning; it never stays the same. He and his colleagues were responsible for experimenting with algorithm changes that would increase the time people spend watching videos, thereby seeking higher advertising revenue.

The algorithm is also circulated on other portals and other social networks. Both search engines like Google or Bing, as well as the most popular social networks (recognized and even lucrative, such as Facebook, Instagram, Twitter, and TikTok), use complex algorithms to decide which videos and which playlists to recommend to their users, especially in what positions to show them and which ones to prioritize.

They are called recommendation algorithms, and YouTube is no exception. It also uses its complex algorithm.

The YouTube algorithm and its effects are crucial. The YouTube algorithm is something that intentionally determines and even motivates users to go through certain videos and channels to continue within YouTube.

Inevitably, it positively or negatively affects YouTubers who upload their videos and expect them to have as many views as possible to monetize them. You might be surprised to know that, at least on YouTube, the majority of visits and views are the result of the recommendations of its algorithms, about 70%, according to YouTube product director Neal Mohan.

YouTube has recently implemented the use of AI on its servers to determine what are the "best" videos for users, something Netflix has long implemented with its millions of customers around the world. It is very beneficial for companies that use artificial intelligence to learn about user preferences and achieve automatic recommendations that keep them consuming hours on their sites.

However, they also manage to reinforce what they already like and thus create an addiction that allows little to explore or see other points of view.

At this point, you must want to know if there is anything beyond recommendation for the algorithms. According to studies, these recommendation algorithms also benefit videos with controversial and extreme content.

At the same time, this can lead many people to a vicious circle of content that, at times, creates radicalization and partiality regarding sensitive issues such as politics, religions, or stereotypes. This YouTube algorithm, for many years, has been creating mistrust, problems, and conspiracy theories.

On occasions and expert analysts' opinion, it manages to alter the course or perception of massive or highly important events in current times, as was the case in the Presidential Elections in the United States.

More than 90% of the recommendations of the YouTube algorithm were in favor of videos of the Republican candidate, Donald Trump. With this, a minimum percentage was left for its main contender, Hillary Clinton.

Do not end up on the wrong side of the Rabbit Hole

A 10-year-old girl uploads a video to YouTube, where she plays in the pool at her home with a friend. Her mother, Christiane, leaves her, thinking of it as something innocuous. An innocent way to keep the memory of a day of fun. However, within a few days, she discovers that his daughter's home video has over 400,000 views and (rightly so) freaks out.

This is a paradigmatic case collected by the New York Times from a Harvard investigation that reveals how the YouTube algorithm is guiding users who have consumed erotic content through – the video suggestion and recommendation system – towards content in which children appear scantily clad or half-naked.

As in the case of Christiane, according to research conducted by the Harvard Berkman Klein Center for Internet and Society group, most of these videos are uploaded by the children themselves (and sometimes by their parents) innocently, looking to share their home videos with family and friends.

The discovery of this YouTube behavior has been made accidentally. Harvard researchers were studying the impact of the social media platform on Brazilian society when they discovered this disturbing behavior of the platform. This is not the first controversy to which YouTube is subjected to minors.

An investigation by YouTuber Matt Watson was translated into a video in which he revealed how pedophiles used this type of video of teenage and prepubertal children to communicate with each other.

These degenerates used the videos' comments to indicate the exact minute and second in which carelessness occurs with the clothes and refer to other videos, external pages, and non-YouTube social media groups in which to exchange material pedophiles.

YouTube was forced to dismantle the comments in response. Even though YouTube cut short its scandal by curbing these videos, the algorithm that automatically guides user navigation and causes many to end up in these prepubescent videos when, initially, they were consuming content of a different nature, according to research from Harvard.

According to the authors of this research, it is not that YouTube purposely wants to promote this content.

It leaves this task in the hands of an automatic algorithm that seeks to continue consuming videos on its platform through a "disturbing" recommendation system. The researchers explain that the path in which YouTube recommendations guides users is progressive.

In this way, to a person who was consuming erotic videos of adult women, the algorithm would guide them through others of younger and younger women. It will go through videos of women dressed in children's clothes looking for a sugar daddy or videos of girls under 20 years breastfeeding their babies.

I am not joking.

Finally, it ended in videos of girls of 5 or 6 years in bathing suits, many of them from Latin America or Eastern Europe. To reach these conclusions, Harvard researchers have performed thousands of simulations with which they seek to map the way YouTube guides its users.

This Harvard research is compatible with the theory (shared by multiple researchers) of the "Rabbit Hole" – a metaphor that refers to the rabbit hole in Alice in Wonderland- according to which YouTube would increasingly recommend more content impressive of a certain topic to keep the attention of its users.

You can capitalize on the Rabbit Hole but never abuse it.

For example, according to this theory, to a user who was watching motorcycle videos, YouTube would recommend videos in which the motorcycles go faster and faster, then races and finally images of shocking accidents.

According to the researchers, the most obvious way to prevent users from ending up in videos of scantily clad children would be to remove videos featuring minors from the suggestion system. An initiative that, as YouTube has responded to questions from the New York Times, will carry out by limiting the recommendations that may put children at risk. According to the company itself, the YouTube recommendation system works through an artificial intelligence system in constant learning that suggests new videos for users to continue consuming content on their page.

Some suggestions, according to YouTube, that provide 70% of the views of the videos, without going into details about how this algorithm works, which is one of the pillars of its success.

Since you are becoming familiar with the world of YouTube and especially learning everything about the algorithm, I felt it was essential for you to learn everything objectively. I took months of effort into researching, talking to people, and coming down with facts for this book, so you do not end up in the same alley.

I am an ardent proponent of the idea that ethical practices and manipulation, by all means, are wrong. It derails the spirit of exactly why you joined the generous platform. It is also wrong and unethical to lead your viewers by manipulation.

It sets a dangerous precedent.

IV

"I Want People to Like, Comment, and Share My Videos and Not Just That But Subscribe Too"

Have you ever wondered why some YouTubers posting a video of munching Cheetos on their couch gain millions of views than most major news sources? Surprisingly, these YouTubers have a concrete audience that companies can only dream of. Literally, PewDiePie's biggest competitor is T-series, a whole giant organization.

All these quirky YouTubers have one thing in common: a concrete audience. Each video follows thousands of likes, comments, and shares. They are always around the corner, waiting to flood a video with engagement. You may also think: "Jenna sits all day doing makeup and has hundreds of thousands of views than you who's talking about climate change," where you get – let's say a few hundred?

You must not forget that YouTubers spend years on building content and a strong fanbase. Everyone starts at zero at some point. The curve is never linear. The key to better engagement on YouTube is making outstanding content and a few other tricks that we will cover in detail in this chapter. *Sit tight, and don't drink.*

Like any search engine, you must index your content to classify it and sort it by relevance. You can take advantage of the way YouTube interprets your videos, making sure they appear on as often as possible. Few people have seen the value of optimizing their YouTube videos. Most geeks like me focus on website optimization and not on video optimization.

This means that 99% of the content you see on YouTube is not optimized. So, if you want to overtake them in the search results. It's pretty easy! By optimizing your videos, you can have tens or even hundreds of thousands of views on your videos. And this, without the need for a single subscriber.

Of course, a small part of the people who watch your videos will subscribe to you. And that's how you can build your YouTube channel.

If you want to touch, aim first

Before you even make a video, it's important to think about your SEO angle. (We have not started with SEO yet, and this chapter has a separate section covering SEO, so don't whine already if you didn't stumble upon it.) When people are on YouTube, they ask the search engine questions.

"How do I make my blue dress fit?"

"Is it normal for bees to sting?"

"How to set up GoPro?"

"How to get the girl/guy you want?"

"Why all lives don't matter until #BlackLivesMatter?"

Your role is to assess the relevant questions that people ask in your niche and to answer them in the best possible way. Next, you need to go see the results of your query and assess whether enough people are looking for that kind of content.

If you mark "How to make money? ", there are going to be several videos of 100,000 views and more that answer exactly this question. Well, that is an indicator that there is a good volume of research. The larger the pie, the easier it is to cut a piece. In short, target the most popular search queries in your niche! You will be surprised how easy it is to get to the first results.

The title of your video is super important!

For obvious reasons, the title of your video is super important. This is probably one of the most important elements in the calculation of the relevance of your video. It is for this reason that it is important to have an excellent title. Yes, it should repeat the words used in the query you targeted, but it doesn't stop there.

In the search results, YouTube calculates the click rate that your video receives! So, you must have a title that strongly encourages people to click. There are thousands of ways to make a good headline, but here is an easy way that works well. Use a number, then an adjective, ending with the targeted search query. You can, of course, mix the order as you wish, depending on the context.

I'll give you some examples:

- Three pork tenderloin recipes that will amaze your friends this summer.

- A ridiculously effective way to get more followers on Instagram.

- Two fun exercises for a 6-pack in less than 30 days.

By using a formula like this, you will not only be relevant to your query but also have a good click rate.

Annotations

As you know, you can add little text bubbles inside YouTube videos. These are called annotations. Most people use it to make short comments or calls to action. Well, it makes me laugh because I still see a very nice way to go up in the search results.

YouTube has access to these bubbles and their content. You can be sure that s/he is using this information to decode the content of your video. If you don't want it to be too apparent and disturbing for the user, well tell yourself that you can put black text on a black background during your transitions.

Add a transcript

Earlier, we discussed that YouTube must guess the content of your video. Why though? Well, as you can imagine, images are much more difficult to interpret than text. Since video content is excessively heavier than text, creating an engine that analyzes, interprets, and indexes each frame from the thousands of videos added every day would be impossible.

It is for this reason that they use other indicators. But what about the sound in this case? It's much lighter than video, and Google already has voice recognition algorithms.

Oh, here comes our old buddy algorithm.

Each video uploaded on YouTube is analyzed, and a transcript is automatically generated. The automatic transcription is not very good if you speak something other than flawless international English.

Fortunately, there is a tool on YouTube that allows you to add your own transcript to the video. If you have scripted your video in advance, as is the case with this video, you just have to upload your transcript, and YouTube will arrange to match the words at the right times in the video. This method gives you a huge advantage over other videos.

Mainly because doing transcription is really long. Few people bother to do it.

Make sure you stay engaged throughout your video

YouTube doesn't just judge the content of your video. It also judges the engagement metrics. Okay, what do I mean by that? Well, it's like on the web. If the visitor goes for a few moments to your site and then immediately leaves to return to the search results, Google will deduce that the content did not meet the visitor's expectations.

Similarly, YouTube analyzes how much time a person spends on your video. If you have a video that lasts 8 minutes and most people watch 6, you will have an excellent engagement score, and YouTube will not hesitate before showing up in the search results.

However, engagement metrics include much more than average viewing time! When people leave comments on your video, it's another clue to YouTube that your video is relevant and interesting. It will, therefore, take into account two things:

1. The percentage of people who view and leave a comment.

2. The context of the comments.

You have to do everything to get comments in your video. Ask people questions, either directly in the video or through annotations. Comments are always seeded through feedback. Finally, there is the famous little thumb up and thumb down on YouTube to indicate that you like or dislike a video.

Inside your video, it's quite common to ask people to click their thumbs up. You can do this by requesting it directly, or through annotations, such as with comments. Ask them to comment, give their opinions and suggestions. Also, you can specifically ask them what kind of video they want you to make?

Take an example of the channel 'Oversimplified', which narrates historical accounts with funny animations and humorous commentary. The comment section is flooded with people asking to: "Can you do the French Revolution?"; "Can you do American Civil War?; "Can you do the Cold War?"

Add your video to Playlists

Once you've done all of this, and your video is online, there are a few more things you can do to appear even more often on YouTube. On your channel, you can make playlists, genres of groupings of videos that play one after the other.

These playlists act as links between two web pages and indicate continuity between the contents.

You must start by creating a playlist and giving it the name of the search query that you had targeted. Then add not only your video but also a dozen other competing videos with a lot of viewing.

It may seem counterintuitive since you are going to help these other videos to stand out in the search results by doing this, except that it will have the sympathetic effect of displaying your video in the column of suggested videos on the right. So, if the person doesn't really like the content they are watching, they may change to your video!

Never forget the 80/20 rule

When they create content, the biggest shortcoming is that they spend 80% of the time on creation and 20% on promotion. Why? Well, because people are too shy to promote their own content. I say that you have to *freak* that out, spend 20% of the time, create exceptional content, and dedicate the rest of your time to promote this content.

Every day you should send emails to people telling them about your content, you should post your video to Facebook, TikTok, Instagram, and you should leave comments on other YouTubers' channels.

In short, you must be in promotion mode four times more often than in creation mode. From an SEO perspective, YouTube needs information to judge the relevance of your video.

At first, if you let it go on its own, it can be really long before your video builds up enough *momentum*.

On the other hand, when you promote your content, you may attract mentions on blogs, and other YouTubers talk about you.

Create thumbnails that spark interest

You usually only have a fraction of a second to capture the attention of the user and encourage them to watch your video rather than that of their neighbor. Besides the title of your video, the quality of the preview image you create is crucial to trigger the click.

Hence there is great importance in designing an image that illustrates and reinforces the subject of your video. 'Vice' is an example to follow: VICE's greatest success is a video entitled "First Animal to Survive in Space" and optimized using a clear and attractive miniature.

Just keep in mind a few basic rules regarding the size of your thumbnail, as it will also be used as a preview of your video when someone shares it on their site. Google recommends the following features:

- A resolution of 1280X720 (a width of 640 pixels minimum).

- Favor image formats such as JPG, GIF, BMP, or PNG.

- Do not exceed 2MB.

- Favor a 16:9 format.

Another example is 'Casey Niestat'. He always puts thumbnails that draw people's interest. Look at the thumbnails on videos like "You Can't Wear That To A Wedding."

Integrate call-to-action (CTA)

When someone watches your video and leaves, it's often because you haven't allowed them to interact and engage with your channel. This is where the Calls to Action feature of YouTube comes in. There are four main ways to get the user into action: subscribe, see more videos, like the vide, share the video, and comment. YouTube offers several options for embedding CTAs within your videos:

Speak directly to the spectator. It's a type of video where you speak directly to the viewer to tell them what to do.

The "End- cards"

The cards are notifications that serve to promote your brand and other videos on your channel. They are cool because they let users click directly on them. If users do not like it, they disappear. On the other hand, the final screen allows you to direct your audience to your next video when the current one is finishing, or directly invite them to subscribe to your channel. Both are very effective and increase the click rate if they are combined with a call to action that you can make verbally at the same time in the video.

Example!

In his video, titled "Intensity," Casey Neistat talks about a movie he made for Nike and refers to it through a card and a verbal call to action.

Allow and encourage people to "embed" your videos

When you upload videos to your YouTube channel, you choose between allowing or prohibiting the publication of your video on other pages via "embed codes". These codes allow third parties to share your videos by posting them on their website, blog, channel, etc.

It's a remarkable way to gaining visibility. Remember to specify that you want to be credited each time your videos are republished. To manage the sharing options, go to the "Video Manager" then select the video for which you want to activate/deactivate the integration. Click on Edit. Reach Advanced settings, and in "Distribution options", check/uncheck the 'Allow integration' box. Finally, click on "Save changes".

Think of the "InVideo Programming" functionality

This YouTube functionality is too rarely exploited. But it is nevertheless a good way to introduce moments of engagement in your videos. It helps viewers navigate to other sections of your YouTube channel. It allows you to do two things:

- **Promotion of video content:** It's the perfect option if you want to promote a particular YouTube video. This allows you to display within a video a thumbnail of the video you want to promote

- **Branding watermark:** This option allows you to embed a logo or an image on all YouTube videos in your channel. The cool part of this option is that your viewers can directly sign up for your YouTube channel by hovering their mouse over your logo.

Allow YouTube to use your videos to promote them

When you're signed in to your YouTube account, you can select one of the videos in your channel for YouTube to select and promote it to its users.

It's completely free.

But of course, only YouTube decides whether to use your video. It remains, however, an effective means of gaining visibility, without cost or any action on your part, except to upload the video of your choice.

Create a series of weekly videos

If you know that every Friday, you will be able to see a video on a subject that interests you, you will probably be inclined to subscribe to the YouTube channel in question. Creating a series of videos on a specific theme at regular intervals is a great way to gain subscribers. It is also a very good technique to entice people to watch the other videos that you broadcast, and therefore to gain views.

Structure your video

Create a clear and interesting narration. Clarify at the beginning what you are going to tell. Develop it and make a brief conclusion at the end. Try to guide the viewer to maintain their interest and attention with the passing of the minutes, speaking in a close and easy tone. You should consider these premises before and during the recording, as well as in the edition.

Optimize long content

This is one of the most important points to ask yourself if you are offering the content of considerable durations. Do not be surprised if your video does not accumulate many views when it exceeds 10 or 15 minutes. The impatience of the Internet user is well known.

So, even if you treat a subject that arouses a lot of interest, it is highly recommended that you create small promotional pieces that serve as a hook and that faithfully summarize the content of the longer videos. This will create good expectations, and it will give more movement to your channel.

Also, try to divide a long piece into several shorter ones and link them together using annotations. You can also do it by including links in the video description that lead to certain time codes. You have to be very clear so that the viewer does not get lost and knows what he is going to see at all times.

Take care of your channel

The health of your channel will depend on the regularity with which you publish videos. Consistency is always an inescapable factor if we want to acquire some relevance and authority in any social network. Encourage subscription as much as possible, since it is a factor considered when determining the importance of one channel or another, within YouTube, and always keep in mind to encourage the participation of your viewers.

Have you seen 'Epic Rap Battles of History'? They have made Rap battles featuring some really famous people. Steve Jobs vs. Bill Gates rap battle. That's how you do it.

Technical production

Although it may seem like a lie, making a video with good quality is one of the simplest things in this process. It requires a little investment and some time to handle the four essential devices and programs. Once you have reached this point, you can focus on what is really going to make a difference, some useful content.

I am not going in detail about what is needed to make a good video from a technical point of view because we have already done that in previous chapters. Each production has its needs, and we must adapt to the product we want to create. Try to make the video look good in terms of light, make the sound as decent as possible, and spend some time thinking about editing the recorded material to make it as fun, direct, and profitable as possible.

At this point, you should bear in mind that the viewer is not going to wait long for your video, so save them logos, presentations, and endless intricacies, go straight to the content, which is what you have come to look for.

You can help yourself with some music to make your content more enjoyable, especially for long pieces, occasionally breaking the monotony. Try to record at the highest possible quality and at the largest frame size that your computer allows since all online video platforms accept content in High Definition (1920×1080 or 1280×720).

Adapt to the format

Creating for the internet gives us (almost) total freedom when deciding what to do, how to do it, etc. They are all advantages. However, try to learn from your mistakes. You have a powerful tool that will give a lot of the information you need to improve: YouTube Analytics.

Apart from the number of views, the geographical disposition of our audience and some other data that you should review from time to time since they can help you a lot to adapt your YouTube Global content (it can tell you if you should start subtitling your pieces in another language, for example).

I want to focus on audience retention data. When does my video stop being interesting? Is there a clear point at which a large percentage drops out?

Is there a point where everyone goes backward? Is it because it is good or because the sound or the image is bad and lost? It is easy to check. You only need a few reproductions to make a reliable average of no more than 200. Take a walk every so often to check this type of thing.

Make YouTube videos short

When I started working in video-marketing, I realized that there is a commonly known golden rule: your videos should not last more than three minutes. And the reason for this? Well, because video engagement is strictly linked to its duration. So is your potential customers' ability to view the entire video and understand what you are trying to sell them.

The average video views drop dramatically after the first 2.5 minutes. The first tip is to create a well-organized video. Otherwise, you won't get to any of the first YouTube pages with long and boring videos.

There are several types of videos, and the explanatory ones are the most effective: they use a brief introduction to present the problem for the first few seconds and then offer a possible solution.

Finally, *monetization.*

Introduce the brand and explain why people should choose this product or service among the competition to solve your problem.

The power of good friends

When you upload a video, YouTube positions you from the third or fourth page down. If you want your video to sneak onto the first page in the first days, I will tell you a trick that works: Ask about ten friends to search for your video by adding the keyword assigned to it to the YouTube search engine. Each one must use different IPs or Internet Protocols. When they find the video, they will have **to** play and watch it (even if they are with other things) until the end or at least up to 80% of the video.

When they see the video, it would be ideal if they like it, leave a comment, and even share it from the same platform.

Why this?

YouTube is a robot, and if in the first hours of uploading your video it detects that even when it is hidden among its pages, people start to see it, share it, leave comments and like it, they will understand that it is being relevant and will begin to position you higher and higher.

This will lead to more views, more subscribers and the ball will start to grow.

Activate the magic link

This trick's objective is none other than to considerably increase the number of subscribers.
And how?

Well, very simple, I am going to pass you a link where you only write the real name of your page on YouTube, in the blank space between "/" and "?" Beware, only the name.

The magic link: https://www.youtube.com/user/?sub_confirmation=1.

If you insert this link in all your social networks, a high percentage of the people who access it will become a subscriber to your page because the first thing they will see is a popup with the button to subscribe to your channel.

Nickname your followers

Your YouTube channel is not about you just making videos. It is you and followers in the same boat. Therefore, you must involve them in what you are doing. Use phrases like "we are going to make it," or "we are going to be very big". Involve your followers in what you do directly. Give them love, dammit, it doesn't cost that much.

A good way to get this involvement is to name your audience. Troy Sivan calls his audience "Troublemakers." Todrick Hall calls his audience "Toddlerz." Grace Helbig – "Gracists," and Hanna Hart – "Hartosexuals."

Make a channel trailer

The best way to do this is to create a channel trailer and include it on your main page. This is the way people will get to know you and your channel. It's a clever way to hook your audience. You have a few minutes to give them a complete outlook on everything your channel stands for. Check out "THE TRY GUYS | Channel Trailer" for inspiration.

You can use this channel trailer to incorporate it on the homepage or put one of your best videos to put there. The video will truly milk views. For example, check out JennaMarbles' "My 200th Video".

"Give Me All You Got on YouTube SEO"

Whether you debut as a YouTuber or aim to retire PewDiePie, you often wonder why your videos do not rank in the search results?

Let's understand what you can do.

Treat your YouTube channel like a website

Conceive and build the main page of your YouTube channel as if it were the website's home page. It is about transforming the homepage of your video channel into a web cover. It will be the one that receives the greatest number of links. It happens to people.

Without going any further: people link more to their YouTube channel than to my own website. Why does that happen? Because their videos are on their channel and, therefore, all the content well compiled and accessible is there.

Create a custom header

In addition to logically personalizing it, your header must bear your name or that of your brand, and the motto or slogan that transmits your message. In the case of the speaker Simon Sinek, we see that he abounds in the concept of "inspiring" people and asking questions (Why?). To make people think and reconsider.

We will select our best videos, and we will post them on that cover. They will be the ones that will receive the most visits, will have the most time to play, and will receive the most link juice. By highlighting and pinning a video, YouTube will automatically suggest that video to you while playing other videos. This will make it easier for the user to continue viewing the rest of your pieces and increase their session viewing time.

Both things come in handy.

We will choose to fix those videos that attack the strongest keywords (usually the guides or tutorials), and we will place them above all. We can plan them so that they have the most interesting keywords within their category.

Below those videos would be the playlists, which can also be positioned for powerful keywords related to our channel's main theme.

When creating your playlists from a Search Engine Optimization point of view, you must enter a text that talks about what is going to be offered. Take advantage of that description to target the target audience of your channel and to attack possible "long tails" since playlists are specific series within your general content and can easily rank for those keywords.

The playlists are going to be the standard-bearers of your production on YouTube.

Interlinking on chain

Within each category or playlist, we can even chain interlinking between the different videos. This will make it easier for people to jump from one video to another and from one topic to another without leaving your channel.

This concept is what we would apply between our videos within each playlist. And among them, we could also do it.

YouTube seeks to offer more and more variety in its results, to give greater heterogeneity. Just like Google. Its search engines become more similar every day, which is not surprising considering that Google bought the video platform now more than ten years ago.

The 15 seconds of gold

You must be very clear about the importance of the first 15 seconds of your video. It is the average time a user can endure to see if they are interested or not in what they are seeing. You have to catch them from the beginning, so you have to put all the meat on the grill in that critical period that is the start of your video.

What do you have to offer in such a short space of time so that the viewer does not leave?

1. Posing the problem or need that a certain group has (for example, "Are you a private teacher and you don't have enough students?", "Can't make it to the end of the month?")

2. Introduce yourself and try to convey your credibility, show that you know what you are talking about, either because you are a recognized brand or because you have worked hard in that field.

3. Advance that you are going to solve those problems in this video.

SEO is not just about keywords but also the context.

Choose the ideal video-keywords for YouTube, and *Google*

The choice of keywords for your video will be different from how you do it on your blog. Many of the visualizations of your videos will come to you from YouTube's suggestions to users. To select which are the keywords of your video, start by investigating your niche. You have to keep in mind that something that has many searches on Google may have few on YouTube or vice versa.

Once you find some interesting keywords and with a minimally decent monthly search volume on YouTube (from 300 onwards), you should check if those (video keywords) also yield results on the first page of Google.

If not, you will have a difficult time positioning yourself in the most used search engine in the world.

Every day, Google prioritizes YouTube videos in its results, even though it is in the "Everything" section and not in the "Videos" section.

In which cases does this occur? There is no official guide in this regard or anything similar. It usually happens with searches in which we ask Google what something is, how it is done, with tutorials, with reviews of products or services, and logically when we search for the word "video" plus "whatever." For example:

If you find some good keywords for your video, you can capture traffic on this channel and directly on the first page of Google.

A full-blown 2×1! It compensates for the effort, right?Let's see some methods to achieve good video keywords.

YouTube search engine suggestions

The operation is like in Google. You type your keyword, and then the bar shows you suggested results. This is nothing other than the usual searches related to your keyword that people do. In other words, information that is worth its weight in gold.

YouTube Analytics Stats

Nor do you need to leave YouTube to find good keywords. With little activity generated by your channel, the platform will show you statistics that include the keywords for which our videos are ranking naturally.

It is as simple as going to your channel's dashboard and clicking on analytics. Within the large drop-down menu, you will see traffic sources and, in turn, YouTube Search. And *tachán*, there you have the keywords for which you are positioning.

With that, you can optimize an existing video with some of those keywords that you did not think about at first, but that has come upon the fly. Simply by adding that keyword as a tag and incorporating it into the description of the video, you will be able to give it a push so that it appears in the first positions of that keyword by which it had already started to upload by itself. Another option is to create another video from scratch around that keyword. This second option is better. It will rank better if directed exclusively to that keyword than if it shares video with others.

Well, with all this, we would already have our well-chosen video-keywords. Let us now go with specific techniques to achieve engagement.

Human interaction in positioning on YouTube

Others call it social cues. For me, they are human interactions, which is what they are. You offer something and that something generates a reaction in others. In the case of YouTube, it can be expressed in different ways. The most common and valued is the comment on the videos.

Off-Page SEO for videos

Five hundred hours of content is uploaded to YouTube every minute. I repeat every minute. An atrocity. And the number continues to grow year after year. This means that the competition is more than greedy for any subject.

Thus, in addition to applying the guidelines we have seen so far, we must also promote our videos outside of YouTube and build their link building based on their keywords.

As with any other content, the more links your videos get, the better positioning they will have in Google searches. Let's see how we can work the SEO Off Page of our videos.

Tags

The labels or tags are keywords that are used so that YouTube can recognize the theme of the video and on what topic or keyword you are focusing on. These are not visible to the user, enhancing the video's visibility concerning the YouTube search algorithm.

Oops, the algorithm again.

You can add up to 500 characters in the labels, so take advantage of them all. Make sure you include your keywords and that they are relevant to the video. Tags are a good resource to add those additional keywords that enhance the strength of your video.

But if you need any help with your tags, you can always look at what the competition is doing with extensions like Tags for YouTube. This will be especially beneficial when it comes to appearing in suggested videos from users who watch videos from your competitors.

Optimize your CTR

You must be attractive to the users so that they come and stay in your video. It does not matter how good your content is if the invitation is not striking.

Still, there was a time when this technique became very popular without falling into the clickbait with low quality or false content. Still, YouTube began to penalize this because it generates a long and bad user experience. This is the first step to improve SEO on YouTube.

The Clickthrough Rate (CTR) is the percentage of YouTube users who have seen the thumbnail of your video and have decided to click on your content. You already know the two basic pillars to improve your CTR: The title of the video and the thumbnail.

A word from a YouTube expert

YouTube experts know different strategies that can be applied to any channel that wants to start on the right foot or increase the number of views quickly.

This is the case of Derral Eves, one of the most recognized video marketing experts – and on the YouTube platform – in the United States. Eves exemplifies his knowledge with the success he has reaped on his channel, with close to 600,000 subscribers. Such relevant brands have also hired him on the platform as Red Bull, American Airlines, and Adobe Software.

He argues that YouTube especially promotes those videos that are consumed for more minutes: a video of a quarter of an hour in duration is of little use if most of them close it after a couple of minutes. It is preferable to upload a 2-minute video whose content is consumed in its entirety. The original video will go up in the ranking and gain visibility if the user goes to see another video from that video. Hence, it is essential to capture the attention of users at the first moment of contact. It is preferable to upload a 2-minute video whose content is consumed in its entirety. For this reason, it is essential to capture the attention of users at the first moment of contact

One of the main tips Eves offers is to "hook the audience" during the first few seconds of the video. Most video consumers abandon it if, after the first few seconds, the subject, the person, or the video's quality has not sufficiently attracted them.

For a video to have millions of views, it must be well defined and easy to find. For this, SEO must be pampered. A detailed and reliable description of the content, labels, audio transcription, and, especially, a descriptive and attractive title in addition to an image (or thumbnail) that creates immediate interest.

Another of the most common recommendations is the one that refers to charisma. You need to have and show certain energy, an intention that is demonstrated in the inflection of the voice, the corporal attitude, and, often, that naturalness does not come out the first time. It takes practice to gain the necessary confidence that will then unleash a more dynamic and authentic style.

Finally, it is necessary to consider the launch times of the videos, try to make them join the social conversations that are being born every day (fads and trends to which they can contribute their content), as well as maintain a certain regularity and consistency of style that conforms a solid base of followers.

V

Instagram for YouTube

Instagram is undoubtedly one of the social networks that have surpassed expectations in recent years. When it appeared in 2010, it was a social network for those who liked to post photos (practically square) and exclusively on IOS. Today, it has become a powerful communication tool that is bringing more users every day.

This social network is opening more and more space for ordinary people to become content producers and true digital influencers. It has new resources and more and more users. To get an idea, Instagram hit the target of 1 billion active users in 2018, with a growth of 5% per month. Since then, it has maintained a steady position.

With so many users, surprising growth, and the ease of producing content, Instagram is a great way to attract your target audience to other channels.

Difficulty to stand out on YouTube

Like Instagram, access to YouTube grows every day, and many are producing content for this platform.

That's where Instagram comes in. A great way to start promoting your channel is through the social networks you already use. Instagram is perfect for placing previews of videos in production, photos of what will be shown on the channel, showing a little of your daily life, and communicating with your followers.

In this chapter, we will cover facts about promoting your YouTube channel through Instagram. We will also learn of things that can be done through Instagram that can help you bring traffic to your YouTube channel.

A brief overview of what you can do

You can do polls and questions which are nice to engage the audience.

Instagram has these features that are great for finding out what your followers want to watch, getting closer to you, making criticisms and suggestions. This way, you have a better chance of communicating with the public and getting the content right.

Tease a little. Make your followers curious.

You should make your followers interested in your videos, so make posts to anticipate what will be shown to the public without much detail. Post a photo of an object that will appear, a video showing the progress of editing, someone, or some special place in the recording to generate this curiosity.

Thus, your Instagram follower will have greater chances to go to YouTube to see the video in full when you announce that you posted on the channel.

You can always create a follow-up link to your video.

When making the video available on YouTube, don't forget to include the link in your bio. Your "bio" is the only place where the link is clickable, and that is why it is the best place to direct your followers without much effort. So, add the link and let everyone know in the stories, for example, to click there and watch the new video.

Also, remember that Instagram is a great tool for testing content. When posting a photo or video in the feed or even in the stories, it is possible to see the reaction of people with comments, likes, and messages via direct. If a certain subject generated many questions and many likes, for example, it might be a good time to make a video on the subject.

Of course, there is no magic formula to become a YouTuber overnight, and it requires a lot of effort and dedication. These strategies that I pass on are simple things that can be done without investment by just being creative and listening to your audience.

A quick guide to posting YouTube videos on Android and iOS

It is possible to publish excerpts of YouTube videos simply in Instagram Stories, even if there is no integration between the platforms. Although the social network does not allow you to access a file directly from Google's servers, you just need to record your phone screen to show videos to friends without resorting to links.

The procedure is simpler on the iPhone since iOS has a native screen recorder. Android phone users, on the other hand, need an auxiliary application. Observe how the technique for sharing YouTube videos in your Stories works.

How can you put a YouTube video in Stories on iPhone using a screen recorder?

First things first. The iPhone screen recorder is in the iOS shortcut panel, but it may not always be available for use. To check, go to Settings and tap on "Control Center." Then go to "Customize controls"

Next. Check that the "Screen Recorder" function is in the first aisle. If you do not find it, look up in the list and activate the shortcut by touching the green button

Hang on. With the screen recorder properly working, open the YouTube video you want to share and place the phone horizontally. Open the Control Center with a swipe from bottom to top and start recording on the recorder button. Right after that, play the part of the video you want to share.

Then, go back to the Control Center option and tap the recorder button. The video will be saved to your iPhone's photo gallery.

Bingo! From there, just open Instagram Stories to find the recorded video in the list of available media items to share. Open it and use the empty spaces to decorate with stickers and Instagram texts - only if you want to. In the end, send it to friends with the option "your story."

How to put YouTube videos in Stories on Android using a screen recorder?

First things first. Download and install the app on your phone. When opening it for the first time, tap "Skip" at the top and then "Continue" to grant the necessary permissions. This is always the case for every foreign app.

Next. On the main screen, find an icon or option which allows you to screen record.

Hang on. In the first use of the recorder, it is necessary to grant additional permission to capture the audio from the cell phone.

Then, in sequence, your choice of the app will display a floating menu to activate the recording. Then, put your phone in landscape mode and play the YouTube video you want to share. At that moment, tap the button to capture the image and sound and let the app record.

Getting there. Track the time on the footer icon. When finished, tapthe stop option, and it will cease recording. You will find the video saved to your gallery,

Bingo! Finally, access Instagram Stories and open the media sharing menu (swipe from bottom to top). Select the video you just shot, embellish it with the app's editing features, and share it with your friends.

"I am lazy. I don't want to screen record. Can't I simply download like I download my entire world from the internet?"

For you to post a YouTube video on Instagram without screen recording, you must first download the video from YouTube. Since you cannot do this directly through YouTube, you will need to use a YouTube video downloader.

The first thing to do is visit YouTube and copy the link to the video you want to use. Copy and paste the link into your YouTube video downloader.

Then, open Instagram on your phone and press the "Add" icon.

Import the video file from your gallery and share it on your Instagram Stories.

Why even bother sharing YouTube videos on Instagram?
The key is to make your videos more personalized, and it can be done through Instagram.

As a content creator, you need to get your viewers' attention to watch your videos and follow your channels. For you to promote your videos quickly, it is important to turn your videos into Stories to attract the attention of your followers.

It can help you attract more followers and, therefore, more subscribers as well.

As we all know, most people make videos to entertain their followers, publicize their products, or even make a tutorial. It is important to know how to put a YouTube video in Instagram Stories to make your video funnier or more attractive.

You can also create a promotional trailer.

You can make a trailer to share on your Instagram Stories and use it to promote your main video. You can also create a teaser that tells a little about what you intend to present to your followers.

"I want to promote my channel on other networks. I mean, isn't Facebook the biggest thing out here?"

Let's learn some numbers here.

According to the study carried out by the companies, We Are Social and Hootsuite, Facebook was still the platform that, in terms of the number of users, beat the rest (about 2.2 billion monthly active users). At the same time, Pinterest was placed in the queue with just over 200 million.

Does this mean that we should focus our recruitment efforts on Facebook? The answer is a resounding NO. The only trend shared by social networks is the weight that stories are acquiring, to the point that less informal pages, such as LinkedIn, have also targeted the car.

Another important factor, also analyzed by the same study, is the potential reach that each network has to impact on a predetermined age group and gender. From this, some interesting conclusions are drawn: Instagram is the most feminine network of the three since women represent 50.3% of the total. And it is also the youngest network. 64% of its users are concentrated between the ages of 18 and 34.

Facebook is a network where 57% percent of its potential users are male. Besides, the average age of the public is significantly higher. The age range between 18 and 34 years is 57%, 7% less than his brother Instagram.

Finally, Twitter is, without a doubt, the most masculine and mature network of the three. 64% percent of its users are male, and 53% are between 25 and 49 years old.

On the other hand, the most demanded video contents are series, cinema, and music, as well as sports, science, adult content, cuisine, and beauty, which means that we find different targets and different types of audiovisual content to promote.

Instagram has become the man orchestra for content creators. Also, we should not lose sight of it since it is the social network growing the most in market share (49% of social network users have Instagram).

The good thing about this network is that it has gone from being a social network of "pretty photos" to a key element to connect with our audience closely and directly. Of course, as long as we maintain daily activity on Instagram, with timeless content and, we especially use the stories. Within Instagram, the possibilities of giving visibility to our content are almost endless. In addition to the photos and videos that we can upload to our news section and the stories, the image network par excellence offers the following options:

Featured Stories: Now, it is possible to save the featured stories so that they remain highlighted in our profile for as long as we want. Featured stories are great for maintaining the visibility of our favorite content.

Links to videos in the biography of the profile or the menu of stories: It is a practice that is increasingly used to link to videos and allows the user to see the full video.

We can also upload snippets of the YouTube video to the feed and link to its URL.

Instagram TV: Instagram TV is a format that allows creators to upload long videos (up to 10 minutes) and, also, it is intended to be consumed from the mobile, therefore, in a vertical format. Be careful, because unlike stories, Instagram TV videos do not disappear after 24 hours. We'll get back to IGTV.

If you also have enough resources, you can buy advertising to promote some of your publications.

You can take advantage of all these formats to upload previews of your video, extra material such as image galleries with photos from the shoot, false shots, that incite the user to want to see more. Always keep in mind that videos have a high power of attraction and of creating links with your followers.

Although it is true that from Instagram you can capture all kinds of traffic, if your YouTube channel is related to lifestyle, contests, gaming, tutorials of all kinds (beauty, recipes, decoration) or very segmented products and services, you will get traffic and engagement with relative ease.

Instagram stories are your greatest chance to promote the channel and generate traffic

Among your options, what works best are usually Instagram Stories. Use Instagram Stories to share experiences, reflections, your day to day progress. In short, to speak face to face (or face to screen) with your audience. And remember that there are about 300 million daily users for your content! Users, moreover, are very willing to consume video content.

Promoting your channel is a mix balance between promotion and building an authentic and genuine connection with your audience.

For one thing, you should delve into marketing tools, share your work, and encourage the audience to show their support. You have a big opportunity to relate to your audience on a human level: show your personality, be honest with them, and share enough to enter your world and understand it.

It is a difficult balance. Fortunately, Instagram has a vast array of features that allow you to wear outfits simultaneously. As we have seen, there are two major functions to share on Instagram: news feed and stories.

Your feed is specifically the area where your videos will live permanently. Many people are extremely cautious about curating their feed to fully reflect their brand and personality.

They only stay awake for 24 hours. So, this is where you can open a little more and play.

Add stories on Instagram by tapping the camera icon in the top left corner of your Instagram home page.

You also have a plethora of options ranging from simple text posts making announcements, showing your stance, saying anything, to posting photos (screenshots of videos), live streams, make those boomerangs, and post snippets of videos. You can add fun filters by tapping the emoji on the right.

If you want to upload screenshots from your videos or excerpts of videos, just tap the image icon on the left side. Once you have what you should post, you can modify it using filters of Instagram, text styles and size, popular and custom GIFs, stickers, relevant hashtags, tags, and even draw on them. Click the option to send at the bottom. Choose "Your Story" and share. If you want to add privacy for some reason, do so. Now your story is live for your audience to view. They will know what's going on, on your YouTube channel.

Once you've published your story, your profile picture will have a ring around it, and your story will be viewable by tapping your profile picture. New updates make it viewable anywhere on the network. You can post stories announcing new uploads. This is a great way to remind people or alert them to flock to your channel if they have not turned on the notification button—the bell icon.

So, now that we know how to make your way with Instagram Stories, let's take on the big why. Why should you use Instagram Stories, among other things?

Ever since it launched, Instagram Stories has accumulated over 300 million active users a day, that's much more than Snapchat clocks. I couldn't believe it either. That's not all; the stories can be discovered. Optimize stories with hashtags and geolocations, so that your audience can easily search.

Consider the following formula: (Audience potential + discoverability = an opportunity to promote your content) This formula is key to promoting your YouTube channel with Stories. And who wouldn't like that?

Another great benefit is that a story only stays for a whole day. It will disappear afterward. But you can always save them in your Highlights.

I understand this is rarely a benefit, but consider it for real. When content is going to be live for only the next 24 hours, you don't have to worry about the quality of the production. This means you finally relax.

The content has full liberty to be spontaneous and a one-off thing. It means you can be more authentic, real, and flawed compared to your other face. This is personalization 101, and I cannot stress it enough. We have talked about it immensely in this book, and it continues to assert its importance. Instagram Stories let you personalize stuff, humanize your brand, reach your audience beyond algorithms, and create a real connection. Showing the real side of you allows your audience to relate to you as an individual. They will see who you are. This is essential if you want to stand apart from other content creators of your industry.

From there, the stories are directly related to direct messages. The audience can "Reply" to your story, which you will see when they send you a Direct Message. You can personally ask them, push reminders, and send automated messages about your YouTube activities. This creates myriad opportunities for individual conversations.

Let's discuss some great ways you can integrate Instagram Stories to promote your channel. Instagram polls integrate into Stories and a good way to engage the audience. Stories are a proven method to generate feedback. To add a survey, create any story, and tap the tag icon at the top. Ask what kind of videos you would like your followers to watch? Take opinions on specific subjects? Get feedback on recipes and other stuff that you are broadcasting through YouTube.

Survey responses are customizable (by default, it is simply a "yes or no"). Inquire from the audience which merchandising design they liked; do they want you to do smokey eye makeup; review the newest Apple Watch?

Which product is most _____ (put any adjectives relating to the connotation you have to suggest) which version of the next song you should record, or which content creator they want to see you collaborating with?

These polls can be mature (like a vote on merchandising design) or just as a fun way to interact with your fans. Give it a few hours. You can enter and see the results of your surveys. Simply swipe up while viewing your story to view analytics.

You will be amazed at the insightful information you can get from these surveys. This helps you improve your content and directly fulfill the wish of your audience.

Use emojis to be more interactive in your text

Emoji controls are like polls. They give you a few fun and customizable options. Like polls, you can add emojis control by tapping the tag icon while editing your story. Ask questions as much as you want, choose an emoji, and add it to your video.

Ask your audience what they think of a project you're currently doing with a heart-eyed emoji. Share some sneak peeks. Ask your audience what they want to see in your next mad scientist experiment. Add a control option with the arrow to let them vote on it.

Once fans have had a chance to give their votes, you can swipe up and see the results. You will see the average response in their analysis. You can also use the stories to promote other social channels.

Have you just released a new video on your YouTube channel? Brilliant. Grab a video from the top of the screen or upload a short edit to the video directly into your Insta-story. Use the icon to add a direct link to the video and embed text telling the audience to drop by to watch.

You can also use Stories to link directly to your store if you are running a brand with products or services. Create a short video to let the audience know that a product is officially available for purchase with a direct link to your store, so they can slide in and make a purchase. Or you can do the same for your affiliates.

Make exclusive content for your Stories

Some content creators occasionally share small exclusives only with their Instagram Story viewers to encourage engagement. Try sharing coupon codes for merchandise discounts or buy one get one free deal where fans can get two items for the price of one.

You can also give the first 100 Story viewers early access to some exclusive content. You could share a link to an unlisted YouTube video before making it public.

Posting snippets from videos as posts is also a good option. But there is something you need to know. Instagram has been making a lot of changes to its algorithm lately, and that means some of your followers may not be seeing everything you post in your feed.

A good way to try to increase the visibility of posts is to share a quick advertisement to Stories.

You won't catch them all, but you can get some of the fans who fell for the algorithmic cracks—you 1 – 0 Algorithm

With that being said, your Stories should be a place where you have all the fun. Do not be afraid to try things and be yourself. Share some video clips of behind-the-scenes when you embarrass yourself in front of the chroma or make exclusive blooper reel. If you are inviting people over, you can add a quick interview with them as well. There are so many possibilities out there.

Use stories in a series to create a mini video. Do a mini-review of a piece of equipment you've been testing, and at the end of it, ask them to follow the link in your bio. The link would direct them to your YouTube.

Or even let the audience help you choose outfits for your next meeting. Or pick the next topic for your video. Hopefully, at this point, you have some great fun stuff ideas to post in your Stories. Never forget that Instagram Stories are a place to share information or behind the scenes content and engage a little interaction between you and your fans, so don't think too hard. Don't milk it either.

IGTV – a kickass way to promote your YouTube channel

Like the clear majority of social networks, innovations do not stop. On June 20th, 2018, Instagram rolled out a new extension that allows users to watch longer videos: IGTV. It is now possible to create a separate channel from the feed with videos of up to an hour. The icon appears next to the Direct option and is also available for download.

Like the popular Stories, IGTV proposes to display videos vertically, facilitating their use on smartphones. Another similarity with Stories is that there is no need to choose a channel and select one video at a time: they will be shown automatically after the other.

It is also important to highlight the suggestions according to the user and their tastes, just drag them to the side for options such as "popular videos" and "keep watching," in addition to commenting and sending to friends.

IGTV features highlights for larger channels, intending to attract content creators by giving them more visibility.

"How will IGTV influence my YouTube channel?"

We turn our attention to understanding how the tool works when updates appear on relevant apps like Instagram. So, we can know how it is possible to use Digital Marketing tools to give our audience more visibility.

With that in mind, I tested the app and brought some impressions of how to apply IGTV daily to attract more people to your channel.

One of the biggest advantages of IGTV is the posting of longer videos up to an hour-long, without needing your follower to leave Instagram or go to the "link in the bio" to watch videos. With a longer time than the platform supported, it is now possible to explore more creative and produce richer content.

This will allow you to create a fanbase that you can lure back to your YouTube. It is like an exhibition to get people to know about your gig.

Through videos, you can better show a product, explain your service more clearly, show customer experiences, interviews, reviews, and whatnot. The limit is creativity. IGTV is a great way to disseminate your content. In addition to being more comfortable for those who watch, since it does not require public effort to be used. It is possible to share the content on Facebook as well. Not bad, right?

For your audience to find your content faster, every time you post on IGTV, your profile followers receive a notification for watching your video. When producing relevant content of interest to your audience, with more complete and creative information, your audience will have more notoriety. As a result, the increase in sales lead may happen.

As it is still a recent tool, this is the chance to be a pioneer. It is interesting to see strategies and the possibility to innovate in this tool, creating a direct channel with your client through audiovisual. Producing video content is essential: according to data from Google Video Viewers, in the last three years, internet video consumption has grown by 90.1%. See, I cannot stop pulling out stats claiming the importance of video-based content here.

Online tools change frantically. They make people to always look for new ways to consume and share content all the time. Take advantage of IGTV to show your audience, its differentials, promotions, new products, answer relevant questions from your consumers and produce something relevant to your target audience are some ideas that can bring results to your business. If you don't run a company but host affiliates, you can do the same for them.

Don't forget Pinterest

Have you thought about integrating your YouTube channel with your Pinterest account? If you want to give more visibility to your videos, it is an interesting idea.

We can increase our business and increase our subscriptions when we combine the power of YouTube with Pinterest. Why not harness the power of both platforms? One leader in videos and another leader in the image. And audiovisual content has already been proven to have a strong impact on brand engagement.

The objective should be close to the fact that the user who visits your Pinterest profile does not need to leave to see one of your videos.

Make sure your YouTube video is fully optimized

If we want to take advantage of the traffic coming from Pinterest, we will have to optimize our YouTube title and description to the maximum before pinning your video. Likewise, it is interesting to add any complementary URL to that description that helps the user who views our video and reaches a specific landing page we intend to convert.

Make sure your YouTube channel is optimized and ready for your users to land on your opt-in pages

Once users reach your channel, they may investigate what other videos are interesting to watch and/or share. If they click on the YouTube profile name, they will go to your YouTube channel homepage.

Have a vanity URL, a suitable design (you can include a background image, according to your corporate identity colors), add the logo to your profile, and have several playlists ready. This will help the user to navigate in your content.

These steps are simple but necessary if we want to take better advantage of the traffic we get from Pinterest and almost any other network that provides traffic to our YouTube channel.

Create a specific Board for your YouTube channel

When adding a title to our Board, we must make sure to use a title optimized for SEO, since that board can bring us traffic both within Pinterest and in Google searches. Like I said, and as always, we will have to take a little time to find the most suitable keywords within our sector/niche. Ideally, create boards using keywords relevant to our business.

Surely in each of your boards, you have four or five specific words for that content that will help you position your pins.

Do not forget to add keywords in the description

When sharing a video, do not leave the description that Pinterest offers when describing the content of your pin empty. Take advantage of keywords related to your niche. You have up to 500 characters to complete the description.

Add a link to your blog or landing page

This can be integrated to your affiliates, and you can charge a higher fee from your partners for this offer. If you have a specific landing where an offer or content ready to convert appears, add that URL in your description.

This not only gives options to the user who reaches your video on Pinterest so that they can convert the objective that you have set for yourself, but it will also generate confidence in it. You can add that link not only to your description but also in the link option, so it is interesting to describe your pin well.

Pin all the videos on your YouTube channel

Now that you've added the first YouTube video on Pinterest make sure to maintain a constant flow of updates. If your videos show an increase in views, consider the option to upload all the videos on your channel.

By leveraging our YouTube videos on Pinterest, we can take advantage of what is called a 'double backlink'. Both channels are fed back, and incidentally, we almost certainly improve the traffic on our website.

This is of great interest to SEO since the links created from websites with a good page rank of trust will increase our ranking in natural searches. Pinterest is the 38th most viewed site on the Internet (the 15th most visited in the United States).

Another advantage that this tactic offers us is the possibility of improving our list of YouTube subscribers. Over time, it will surely result in an increase in your database for an email marketing campaign.

VI

"I Want My Channel to be the Most Viewed."

Session watch time is a much sought-after aspect of a successful YouTube channel. But what does it mean? Watch time totals the duration your audience sticks around on your channel by specifics on each video. YouTubers nowadays cram towards techniques and strategies to increase watch time. It is as important as having subscribers in abundance and a sound reputation.

But why do so many YouTubers get it wrong? I am not even going to mention how first-timers overlook this aspect. Increasing the watch time of your YouTube videos lands a vast array of opportunities and is directly linked to monetization.

Watch time is essential because you can have great relevance and place your videos on search engines. I know the most common problem here: having a YouTube channel with good content to share but failing to reach the audience you want and increasing views. Prevent your exit rates and view times from being low with these useful tactics that will increase your relevance on YouTube.

Let's take an overview here.

Being a "YouTuber" is the dream of many. It seems like an easy and fun job. And maybe it is a playful activity. Quality content matters, but there are also many factors behind a successful YouTube channel. Everything has a process and a 'why'. This is why I have analyzed a bit of the element that a video must contain and the best practices for your YouTube channel to start taking off.

Continue reading what I explain everything you should consider before uploading your next video to YouTube. Who knows, maybe in the future, you will be the next fashionable "influencer." You must never stop dreaming.

Many of the famous YouTubers started recording their videos. Now, they most likely have a team and people to help them. Don't worry. You don't need a lot of equipment. It's the last thing you should think about if you're starting, the important thing is to create quality content. The equipment can be acquired over time.

These are the elements that you must validate for increasing watch time of your YouTube videos:

- Define very well what will be the subject of your videos.

- The beginning of your videos, like the first 15 seconds, should be for the best. Something striking for the viewer to stay.

- The name is very important; a good title for your video can attract the attention of potential viewers.

- Describe your video accurately, using keywords. You should always put text in the description.

- Use the appropriate tags. You should sit down to analyze what your video is about and what are the keywords that accommodate it to appear in the searches.

- Share it - without fear - in all possible ways. Even try to send it to all the contacts you have emails from, on all social networks. Look for ways in which they allow you to watch at least one of your videos.

We will cover these aspects in more detail in this chapter.

I will take you through the most useful tips that can maximize your metrics. Bring about the real 'you'. Make them like your content. Subscribe to your channel. Pay attention, and you will see that it is simple. Surely as a YouTube content creator, you have already faced the following question:

What should I do so that my videos are among the first search places and are shared or recommended?

To have the desired success consider the following: for some time, YouTube promoted the channels based on the number of views by videos. However, this changed from 2012 by the implementation of a new algorithm. This algorithm ensured that users had a better experience. *Here we go. The algorithm, again.*

This factor has been a priority for making content viral. Its recommendation property has placed videos in the best positions making them viral trends.

The algorithm was created so that users have access to the most competent and entertaining content. It could reach those who need and search organically for the valuable information that a particular video contains.

With this, users have greater access to content that is similar to what they see. They can learn more about the subject they are looking for. In this case, one of the factors that will make YouTube promote your channel in the search box or the list of recommended videos will be the viewing time.

Viewing time, as I said above, is the number of seconds or minutes that the viewer spends playing the video. This gives you an idea of the type of content viewers actually see, as compared to the videos they click on, and then when they don't get their attention, they drop out. The video format is one of the most beneficial resources to promote products and services. Through video, the message reaches your audiences effectively. They likely respond very well to them since videos incorporate communication, interaction, immediate response, attention, interest, and entertainment.

All said, and considering how important YouTube video is in your content strategy, I present you these useful guidelines that will come in handy to make the changes you need to make to optimize your resources and increase the time of viewing your videos.

You will soon see how implementing these recommendations will help you to get more organic reach, leads, and more views. More followers and subscribers will come to you. People who look for what you provide and who will be attentive to what you publish from start to finish.

The masterpiece is in creating valuable, relevant and engaging content. Ask yourself: What can I do to make my video amazing and catch people's attention?

A video should not extend more than necessary. Be concise and make the content attractive and interesting. Remember that people are looking for an answer and if they don't have it quickly, they get bored and leave.

It is recommended to give a little value in the information that you broadcast within the first 30 seconds or give a preamble to what the video contains.

On the other hand, it is also convenient to put in the description box the topics and seconds in which the video is distributed. Give credit to the data sources you use to avoid violations, demonetizations, or censorship of your work, or copyright claims from others.

If most of your videos are boring, too long, or tedious, then that will be the brand identity you will project to your audience.

Make most of your videos interesting so that you create a brand identity. Branding is crucial for a segment of the audience. If you are a beginner, try to make the videos as short as possible so that your retention and relevance capacity will increase over time, and you can lengthen your videos more.

Remember that the brand you build over time is with patience and effort in making the best videos you can.

Hook them with RELEVANT information

Hook them up from the start.

You can briefly describe what the content will be at the beginning, and it closes with a golden hook at the end. It mentions that you will finally indicate how to win a raffle, a special bonus, or only provide examples, sources, or case studies on how to apply the video's content. In this way, the user will have to see the full video and not skip parts of it.

They see you as they treat you: increase the production of your video

To gain value, credibility, good looks, interest, projection, even credibility - add graphics, images, visuals that can please and entertain your audience. Remember, the human eye reacts based on stimuli, and these resources can make your video more attractive and that users stay longer in it. It is important that you also maintain the energy and attitude that you want to convey throughout the video.

Let's see it this way. If you are in a live performance and your body posture is bent, do you think you will be full of vitality and dynamism to make a long-lasting live performance? I beg to differ.

Your audience perception will not be the most positive. Let's face it. Energy begins to decline, which will be projected to your audience, and they will likely start to get bored. It will get them to leave the video.

Make videos with the necessary duration. Sometimes YouTubers speak to their audiences as if they were addressing their friends. Unless you are Bob Ross and "beating the devil out of the brush" and telling the viewers to accept their mistakes because they are not "mistakes" but "happy errors," you are not supposed to put together long rants. You should relax, not force the action. Let yourself find a comfortable space.

Evaluate how long it takes you to tell gossip or news to your friends, the body posture you take, your look, gestures, tone of voice, and you will know that a video should keep that rhythm. YouTube usually gives relevance to videos for less than 15 minutes. You will see them placed in your recommended videos section. Make a list of talking points and place them in order.

Get to the point from the beginning of the video and provide the valuable content you have been aiming for. In your metrics, identify if videos have lower audience retention. Review the video and identify why people leave and when they do so.

Maybe it's because you lowered the energy you had initially, or the content was repetitive. Do a constructive analysis of the material you created. The comments that your followers leave in the thread also help. Read them; do not take some of those personally because Internet trolls are inevitable. Just filter the opinions that help you improve, and over time you will see how you become their favorite YouTuber.

Keep in mind that what can be measured and analyzed can be corrected. Focus on getting familiar with your metrics and make the small or big changes you require until you reach those peaks of the audience that you are looking for.

Create playlists

To create a better user experience and be able to hook them one video after another, group your best videos in playlists or create a logical and meaningful sequence of the topics you tackle to keep them interesting.

We have addressed this point in previous chapters as well. If what comes next is useful, there will be a greater chance that people will look at more of your product and realize the high value of visual content you offer.

How to do it?

It is very simple. You must optimize your playlist using the function to order the videos. You can drag and drop the video up or down to reorder the playlist. Keep in mind that if your introductory videos are very long or not attractive enough, it is better to delete them so that a viewer is not put off.

At the end of your videos, add a link to the videos that may be of interest or are related to the video they just viewed. You could even redirect them to your playlists, and they will continue to watch your videos, which will increase the viewing time.

Nail the title

Your title must be very precise concerning the content. The title is the first element that triggers interest. It will single handedly sway their opinion on whether to view your video or not. Choose an image that is appropriate with the title, because if you take or give the wrong impression of the video content, the user will probably feel cheated and stop watching the video, which will affect the viewing time.

Try that the title and description of the thumbnail tell a story that manages to intrigue the user to give you the desired click. Make sure both are suitable for the mobile and desktop versions. I recommend you check the retention time of your videos. If the audience exits or closes the video in the first 10 to 15 seconds, your title and description probably need to be changed.

Add cards to your videos and keep them

Take advantage of the automatic replay system and the card of information by emphasizing your followers and breaking down more data about a topic you touch on in your main video.

It is possible to add cards for different purposes. However, to keep your users hooked, I suggest that you add links to your other videos or to your playlists that are of interest to the user. Indicate them when you touch the theme throughout the video and show them again seconds before the end of the video to avoid losing your follow-up from the user.

The key is in the words and phrases

One way to establish or arrive at these long-tail keywords or key phrases is through the suggestions that YouTube provides in the search box. Take into account that these are not just random suggestions but also searches that users similar to yours have made. You can see what type of videos your competitors are uploading and what type of keywords they use to establish your own.

Use of end screens

The final screens are a space that we dedicate to a video at the end. Therefore, when editing the video, we must leave a few "extra" seconds, since we can incorporate elements such as:

- Videos related to the current

- Place a subscribe button

- Shout outs

- Call to actions

- Branded banners

A good example of a final screen would be adding a subscription button with a background that includes an arrow and the YouTuber that encourages the audience to continue consuming channel content.

Also, in YouTube Analytics, we can measure how many clicks we receive on those final screens, and which ones you put on the most visited. This way, you will know if you have hit the videos you suggest on the final screen, or if nobody clicks on them.

"Community" Section

The "community" section of the channels is always forgotten, but it is quite interesting. It is a way to send messages to your subscribers. This message will appear in the user subscriptions tab (in the mobile version). You can put what you want: a reminder that you have uploaded a new video, a poll when they prefer you to post, announce the next video, and generate expectation.

Unlock new videos with goals

Many YouTubers adopt the practice of pushing their viewers to watch videos in exchange for new relevant content. For example, they say: "If we reach 20,000 likes, I upload the next part!" In this way, they encourage viewers to reach that goal to continue consuming their content. You can also treat them to cover a series in-depth, add behind-the-scenes, blooper reels, and some exclusive content.

Put the best comments in each video

Some YouTubers paste the best comments at the end of their videos from users (from the previous video, of course). Stick them up on the final screen.

This is a nice way to build your audience's trust. When they see other viewers' positive comments, they are likely to follow suit. You can add pleasant background music for a few seconds when video prompts the best comments.

And finally, I wanted to announce a great improvement within YouTube Studio that is relevant to this section. It is the control panel for your channel. It turns out that in YouTube Analytics, we can see the "click-through rate" or CTR of your videos, and a message appears in which they warn that the more clicks our videos receive and the longer they watch them, the more times they will recommend us among suggestions.

Therefore, for YouTube to suggest our videos, we must increase the CTR and the viewing time. Retention (the time they watch your video) can also be measured in YouTube Analytics, and thus you will know when your viewers leave or return.

These are techniques that are best added at the editing level. Put the batteries in all areas, and you will see results.

It is also important to interact with other users, that is, respond to comments for greater visualization. But there are other elements that we must take care of.

If you are serious about being a YouTuber, you should think beyond YouTube. It is essential to create a personal brand, and of course, that matter involves investing. Because nothing is free in this life, but it's worth it.

Buying a hosting and a domain to create a blog for your YouTube channel can push you forward. Perhaps your audience is interested in telling you stories or more about your creative process. It's not all about "pretty videos."

The visual theme is everything. You must choose preview images (thumbnails) of your videos that are powerful, that attract attention. It is possible to create them with useful tools available on the internet. Take good care of the details that your channel has a visual impression so that your viewer cannot stop seeing your content.

Videos should also be as accurate as possible, think that the more content you have, the better. You must be constant. So, if a topic is very long, you can create a series of two or three videos, instead of one, which would generate more reproductions. Upload videos periodically, maybe once a week, but never stop being constant.

YouTube is a community. Try to engage with other content producers, seek collaborations with other channels, to get people to know you more.

There is no secret formula for being "famous." This requires work, hard work, sitting down to analyze what works and what does not work. Inspiring yourself works, but copying does not. Take good care of the technical aspect, that is, record where there is good light, try to make the audio as clear as possible if you cannot do it alone, invite other people to be part of your project.

Before continuing with the list, you are surely wondering how these characters can earn money with a social network. Although it seems strange, like on television, they live on brands that guide their channels. Every time an ad appears before a video, rest assured that YouTuber is being given some money to show it. So, there is a team on YouTube charged with making the connections between the creators of the videos and the advertisers.

Of course, for that to happen, you must first have a considerable number of followers (they can be hundreds of thousands, like millions), and, depending on that number, the reach of an ad is calculated. We have already discussed that in the chapters before.

YouTube has already made everything clear so that you can reach your goals. And that is why it tweaks recommendations for your videos to be successful. You have all the rights to the audio-visual material of the video. So, there is the freedom to play around here more and more.

The more views a video has and the more followers a channel, the greater the monetization. As YouTube works with exact and public figures (and there are more and more people who prefer to watch content on this social network than on television), the calculation is more accurate, and the flow of advertisers is greater.

If that were not enough, as they become more popular, some brands prefer to make a more accurate impact and contact YouTubers to sponsor or ask them to feature their products in one of their videos. You can imagine how much it translates into money. Like I said, increasing watch time is the key to monetization.

Yes, it sounds simple. But it is not. Ask these YouTube stars.

Now we will discuss how some of the most successful YouTubers today, with billions of views in total and grossing tens of millions of dollars a year, became successful. I have listed some of the biggest YouTubers with the most follower count. We will take a look into their background, and some astonishing numbers boasting their success. And of course, I will sum up what you can learn from them in one line.

While you are about your journey, you need to know what kind of content has been successful in the past and present. These are use-cases, notable examples for you. You can learn from them some important insights which are essential for your own YouTube plan.

FunToys Collector Disney Toys Review

Formerly known as 'DisneyCollectorBR', this channel has got billions of total visits. It sits at 11.5 million subscribers. It is a channel of a Brazilian YouTuber whose identity is unknown and publishes videos of the opening, assembly, and use of Disney toys while commenting on the details with a soft tone of voice.

It is the favorite channel of many children whose peers ensure that they calm down and entertain themselves with these productions.

*Key takeaway:*Children are crazy. If you are up for it, target them.

BFvsGF/PranksvsPrank (which no longer exists but is massively popular for many reasons)

Back in time, the couple Jesse Wellens and Jen Smith were the celebrity couple on YouTube. I am still not over their breakup. The channel started after Jesse, the boyfriend, tricked Jeana into allowing him to record her while she eats a full spoon of cinnamon.

The video was an instant hit, which did not make a bit of grace to his girlfriend Jeana, and she decided to take revenge by recording a video in which she hit him with a frying pan on the head. From there, it has become a phenomenon of jokes that have been escalating and launched into what we know the most darling couple on YouTube.

However, the couple broke up during 2016 and announced their breakup in a video titled, "A New Chapter." Ever since they both went about their separate channels and are still a YouTube sensation.

*Key takeaway:*Humanizing your content can make a huge difference. Giving your subscribers an up close and personal glimpse into your life and introducing some important people helps you build a fan base.

JennaMarbles

The celebrity boasts 20.2 million subscribers in 2020. Jenna Marbles has long been recognized as a YouTube star since her inception with BarStool Sports, who later changed videos such as "How to Trick People Into Thinking You're Good Looking," "Things Girls Lie About," "How To Avoid Talking To People You Don't Want To Talk To." She is the ideal YouTuber who manages millions of dollars a year, thanks to her videos.

*Key takeaway:*Consistency is key. Being original, owning up to what makes you different and unique pays off eventually. Do not try to be something you are not. Embrace who you truly are and let the world see it.

Rosanna Pansino

This YouTuber currently has 12.3 million subscribers. She is a young chef from Washington who went to Los Angeles to make her way to the gastronomy world. After many unsuccessful attempts at the restaurant guild, she decided to teach her baking tricks on YouTube. In 2011 she invented a channel called 'Nerdy Nummies', recorded in his kitchen where he teaches how to make cakes in creative ways like pokeballs or Disney princesses. In less than a year, the channel reached 60 million video visits, which to date, marks almost 1 billion views. To top it off, she published a book with her recipes and advice and of course, she entered the New York Times list of Best Sellers.

*Key takeaway:*If you are talented or skilled in some way, capitalize on it. Your talent can set you apart, even from competition.

RomanAtwood

RomanAtwood is the heaviest and best-known prankster on social media with 10.5 million subscribers. He became popular for his risky hidden camera jokes like urinating on police officers or challenging people in the street to get an idea of their occurrences.

Thus, in less than four years, he managed to get brands like Nissan to sponsor him without hesitation. As if his joke channel was not enough for him, two years ago, he invented a vlog where he posts almost daily about his life (or whatever comes to mind) and has 15.3 subscribers. While he continues to make his content, he already has his store called Smile More and is planning to make a movie.

*Key takeaway:*Sometimes, it takes courage and pis*ing off a lot of people.

Lilly Singh

Thirty-one years old, Lilly Singh is a Canadian YouTuber, and those who know her better, know her as 'Superwoman', which is what she calls herself on her standup comedy channel on YouTube.

Although she has a degree in Psychology, she started uploading her ideas on YouTube in 2010. Her main videos covered the daily life of a young woman of Asian descent in Canada with humor and anecdotes with brown parents.

Followers and fans soon followed, and in less than two years, star managers like Ed Sheeran and Ariana Grande contacted her to make appearances with her. Today she has her standup comedy set up, and in 2015 she started a trip to Unicorn Island, which has filled audiences in countries like India, Australia, and Singapore.

It all started with a YouTube channel where she currently has 15 million subscribers. She also published a best-seller book: "How to Be a Bawse: A Guide to Conquering Life."

*Key takeaway:*Being comfortable in your skin is important for originality.

Michelle Phan

Fashion and beauty products are heaven for women. This makeup artist's channel remains the one-stop for makeup tutorials and it currently has 8.89 million subscribers on YouTube. Michelle Phan started making tutorials to teach women how-to put-on makeup and the like, and her success was immediate.

She went from being a waitress in a sushi restaurant to being one of the most influential women in this social network. Any tutorial you like is based on your idea. Without hesitation, giant industries like Lancôme contacted her to have their products featured in their videos and eventually launched their line of products called EM Cosmetics.

*Key takeaway:*Do what you love. Do it every day. You will face obstacles, but sticking to what you love and do, is going to make all the difference.

JJ Olatungi/KSI

A British YouTuber, who started his journey on YouTube in 2008 at age 15. To make you angry, this guy makes a living from YouTube videos doing something you do all the time: play soccer video games.

He knows all the tricks that any gamer would like to master and thus became a network authority in a sort of genre that was born from these sites: video game commentators.

His success has been so absurd that he has been sponsored by brands such as Microsoft and FIFA. He even entered the Guinness Book of Records as the person who has scored the most goals in a soccer video game against a computer. But, since it is not enough, he has also been successful as a rapper and even with comedy videos.

*Key takeaway:*If you think you are the best at something, never shut up about it.

Rhett & Link

Two Inseparable friends from school and nerds to the core (or so it seems) are engineers who live from making comedy videos on their YouTube channel, which has 4.92 million subscribers.

They became famous for their YouTube program called 'Good Mythical Morning', a kind of talk show with short dramas and tutorials.

It's tuned in by millions of people daily, like any television show, so much so that they ended up on the CW Network on a show called 'Online Nation', but it was a failure. However, the channel continues to be more alive than ever, and they are called from time to time to collaborate on film and television.

*Key takeaway:*Have a charisma that forces people to stick around.

Lindsey Stirling

This violinist is the closest to a star born on YouTube (and, of course, also a boy named Justin Bieber). She opened her YouTube channel initially called Lindseystompafter after many attempts to take off her career on a record label. She started publishing videos, where she interpreted her material and immediately found an audience on the social network.

The success came immediately: she participated in America's Got Talent, has sold more than 1 million singles online, has recorded two studio albums that have been a hit in Europe with more than 200 thousand copies sold, and has been a winner in the Billboard Awards. Lindsey Stirling has 12.5 million subscribers on YouTube currently.

*Key takeaway:*Never give up on your dreams.

Fine Brothers Entertainment

All the videos about people's funny reactions originate from 'React', the series which created their YouTube channel. Their names are Benny and Raphy, and they are indeed brothers. They grew up in a super-strict Jewish family in Brooklyn and spent their entire lives making videos, among other things, to laugh at themselves.

When YouTube came to the world, they did not hesitate to put together a channel and immediately became the closest thing to a production company intended only for this social network. Since 2004 they have been giving praise and are the gods at the IAWT Awards, something like the Oscars of streaming videos. FBE's YouTube channel has 20.1 million subscribers.

*Key takeaway:*Innovative ideas that can work have huge potential.

Smosh

This pair of friends is the closest to a Saturday Night Live on YouTube, or well before SNL had a channel on this social network. They started messing around making silly things – yes, literally silly things – with webcams in their homes in 2003 and when they switched to YouTube, visits did not stop coming.

They perfected their technique so much that they have created comedy formats about video games, reactions, cartoons, and even have their movie (The Smosh Movie) that was a box office success in the United States. With their work, they have reached three times the goal of the channel with the most subscriptions. Although they are now dethroned, if we add the number of people subscribed to all their channels, they have more than 50 million. The original channel currently has 25.1 million subs.

*Key takeaway:*Production quality and aesthetics go a long way, giving you the edge over others. Never compromise on video quality.

PewDiePie

This skinny Swede is called Felix Kjellberg, he is 30 years old and has a YouTube channel which has earned him a fortune since 2008, mounting videos of something that many watch to kill time: commenting on video games, parodies, roasting sessions, and a whole lot more.

Fully aware of how much trick there is in every video game that comes to mind, he has reinvented himself in every way (even doing comedy while teaching how to play videogames). He has all the records you can imagine: the channel with the most subscribers, the most viewed in history, and the most monetized. And there's you, who was told that videogames are bad for children. PewDiePie has 105 million subscribers.

*Key takeaway:*No one has a secret recipe for success, and PewDiePie's success bears testimony. Hard work, consistency, and originality eventually pay off.

VII

<u>YouTubers And Their Toys</u>

The phenomenon of YouTubers does not stop growing. Already in late 2015, it was said that the video format would be preferred by users in 2016. Now, five years later, other formats are simply considered outdated or too complicated to monetize, given the amount of content in digital form. If we ask 12-year-olds in schools what they want to become when they grow up, some of them will tell you that they want to be vloggers.

What is the vlogger phenomenon, and how do you get profitability from uploading videos to the internet? Let's go by parts, to understand the wonderful world of YouTubers or video bloggers. In addition to being in charge of a vlog, vloggers decide to make specific plans to periodically upload their content on YouTube. Vloggers specialize in a specific topic, which can be very varied, and they create and upload videos on the chosen video platform in different formats. We can find channels for beauty, fashion, cooking, sports, entertainment, travel, vlogger games, streamer games, DIY, technology, marketing, or music.

The formats that we can find in a video channel can be tutorials, interviews, tests, but always in video format. We can find vloggers who make use of social networks and who also have a website, but everything will depend on the strategy they carry and their way of monetization. Video is the format par excellence on digital platforms and social media, for two main reasons:

1. On one hand, people like to read less and less. Usage of the web has brought us the new increasingly "lazy" public.

2. On the other hand, video content is faster to understand and enjoy. It produces more interaction and more engagement with the user.

The user who enjoys the video format is more likely to comment or share, to quickly enjoy the content, and to want or need more content to be able to comment on again. Most people in the world have watched videos by vloggers and have not been able to resist watching one or two more videos.

This characteristic of videos causes a vlogger to generate good content with a content plan and good communication, to create a strong community of subscribers and monetize quickly. Millennials are the ideal target audience for vlogs. According to data from the study of the Network Observatory of the consulting firm The Cocktail Analysis, where over 480 young adults between 18 and 30 years of age were interviewed, more than 59% of those surveyed consume daily videos on YouTube and more than 68% watch branded videos.

In the same study, it is stated that the video format in millennials stands out from the other formats due to its search for permanent stimulation. More than 20% of respondents faithfully follow YouTubers and other influencers ahead of celebrities and movie stars. If your target audience is millennials, be clear that you must make vlogs.

"Okay, I want to dive into the wonderful world of vlogs, but where do I start?"

For some YouTubers, their YouTube channel is a personal or daily space in which vlogs portray personal experiences. It includes their day-to-day life, opinions, rants, etc. in video form. What were known as bloggers have become vloggers. The content marketing strategy presented in the written blog remains the same in most cases, but this time in audiovisual format.

We could say that the rule of "an image is worth a thousand words" is fulfilled in this case. Some bloggers now complement their content with one or more channels with which to be diversified on various platforms and go to various targets.

For example, a fashion blogger may have their blog, their online store, a fashion channel, and one of the daily vlogs. It shows different faces of the same coin, and on all these platforms, different brands can be without conflict of interest, because the target can vary quite a bit.

Be that as it may, YouTube is undoubtedly a proven platform to reach young viewers who have stopped consuming content on television and have moved into the digital world.

What started as another way to consume content became a big trend for advertisers too. Advertisers prefer to interact with their target audience through content that engages, leaving aside the traditional written blogs that with the appearance of the smartphone have become vlogs.

Vlogs generate more connection with the viewer. After all, they are a face to associate with the brand's personality. Also, they increase traffic to the web (a link is usually embedded in the description box of the videos), brand awareness and achieve greater visibility and affinity, as long as the influencers are carefully chosen.

In the lifestyle field, Casey Neistat stands out internationally, with more than 12.1 million subscribers. The content of this daily vlogger is not only a reference for just you, but many international YouTubers consider his work a benchmark. Casey Neistat is chased by global brands and multinationals, offering him sponsorships.

How can you, as a novice vlogger, follow the same footsteps?

Your vlogs must reflect an honest outlook on everything you do. Users must assess if a brand that appears in a video fits with the host and that what is being sold is legit. A shortage that is being seen in recent years are those YouTubers that, in a short period, announce brands from the same segment that are direct competition.

For example, one day, they announce a juice brand talking about all the properties they have, and in a few months, they talk about another juice brand that is also spectacular. Your credibility is undoubtedly at stake with these types of decisions.

The channel must be updated. Vlogs feature periodicity. They are usually daily or at least weekly. There are indeed other modalities in which it is published monthly or at more specific times as special vlogs during the Christmas period. In this regard, we must highlight British YouTuber Zoe Sugg's channel.

Popularly known as Zoella, she posts makeup tutorials and creates vlogs around her lifestyle and the people involved in it. However, at any given chance she features a special segment covering a special occasion.

You must be original and take risks. A vlog must reflect the naturalness of the day-to-day, which is usually very effective and makes the relationship with the consumer more intimate, which is why the recommendation on brands will be perceived differently.

You have to keep in mind that you cannot focus all your efforts on a single platform and, above all, you have to try to be able to directly contact your followers. Therefore, you must have a digital strategy where your subscribers, in addition to subscribing to your channel, follow you on other social networks. You must get them to visit your website or blog to get a mail form or a subscription banner.

In this way, whenever you want, you can contact them to announce a new video, a new collaboration, or a new product or service. The price of your collaboration for a promotional video that you close with a brand or product will depend directly on your community. Your community will include all your followers on social networks, subscribers to the blog, the channel, and your database, and the value of your blog will depend on how large the community is.

Differentiate yourself and stand out among thousands of people who upload unprofessional videos to YouTube. You will think that it takes months of preparation, study teams, analysis, research, right? Most people will feel overwhelmed, but the reality is different. It's easier than you think.

This guide is intended for people who want to make vlogs with a professional touch and without breaking the bank for it. What do you need to start recording better videos? Recording professional-looking videos or setting up a small home video recording studio is within everyone's reach.

"What equipment do I need to start recording my professional videos?"

If we want to be serious about vlogs, we need to cover certain basic needs with specific equipment.

Pro equipment makes the difference between the millions of vlogs that are created every day on YouTube. Also, vlogs created through pro equipment always stand out and gain influence, followers, and views.

On the contrary, if we do not understand the basic needs of recording videos, we will not get professional material, and our videos will have low quality or seed. It makes the viewer lose interest and move on to something else, even if the message is interesting.

For this, I have carefully reviewed options ranging from simple and cheap to expensive and complete pro. Keep in mind that the result will depend on the whole set. It will not help us to record with a top-tier camera if lighting is terrible or the audio is super bad. So, pay attention. Let's start with the most important: how to find the best camera to record your videos? You can most definitely start with a smartphone camera without a doubt and starting with the most basic and cheapest. Many people today own state-of-the-art smartphones with the ability to record videos in high definition. A few high-end smartphones can give youimpeccable video quality. In fact, with the camera of your mobile terminal, you can obtain more than enough quality.

If you have an iPhone, or one of the latest models from Samsung, or other similar quality smartphones, you already have one of the most important things to start recording professional-looking videos. However, generally, a DSLR camera has superior optics and will ensure better quality in both photo and video.

We can consider as basic requirements that you record with a high resolution or Full HD (1080p). Even better if you can in 4K. These are some of the characteristics to consider if we are going to buy a camera to record videos:

A good focus and tracking system, face and eye detection to keep the person's face focused in different modes. This point is essential for vloggers. It has an external microphone input as well. 4K today is not necessary. Especially if your videos are destined for the web.

However, recording in 4K has many advantages, such as quality improvement when resizing to FHD, being able to crop 4K to get new FULL HD planes (as if we had a second camera). You also have a higher level of detail (8MP photo quality frames can be taken).

Do a quick Google search to find out the best cameras on the market today to record professional videos. Remember that the most important thing is to use any available resource and that if our budget is tight, we can start with cheaper options such as recording videos with your mobile.

Do not ignore the sound. There are microphones to record professional audio on videos. Sound is much more important than most people initially think. It is usually the factor that makes a big difference when producing a professional-looking video. Sound is as important (sometimes even more) than the quality of the video image.

Capturing sound with the camcorder's internal microphone is a no brainer. Whenever possible, use an external microphone or an external recorder. The point now is that you can get a good image quality easily, since most cameras or mobiles today record good videos, but the same is NOT the case with sound. If our sound is not good, the video will fail to make the cut.

Lighting – take your videos one step further

You can go out today and purchase a flagship camera, but a camera only captures the light of the scene across. If the scene across is poorly lit or has inappropriate lighting, the result will be bad.

Lighting is a major determinant in achieving quality video and photos.

We are not talking about the amount of light, but rather maneuvering light to create that environment that we want to transmit for the scene to be recorded, and that makes it more understandable. Lighting as a scene is an art and a science. Hence, some professionals are dedicated to this alone and are known as "art directors."

Although lighting is a whole field that you can delve into, there are always a series of basic tips that will help you improve your results a lot. Without a doubt and in most cases, the best light is natural light. You can organize your room to use a window as the main light and a white reflector (a very cheap item that you can find second-hand even for less than $10) to fill light.

Image stabilization – get cinema results in your videos for YouTube

Stabilization is another of those key factors when recording your quality videos and an important feature of production that we will address. There are three types of image stabilization:

- Internal camera stabilization. It can be done via software or hardware, and the latter usually only appears in the most professional cameras.

- Lens stabilization (a little expensive).

- External stabilization (Steadycam, Gimbal, etc.) or a simple tripod.

"How do I find the ideal tripod for my videos?"

If we want to start with the simplest (and cheapest), one of the first pieces of equipment that we should consider is a tripod. Use a table top tripod, but in general, it is convenient to have a proper one with which we can regulate height and adjust stability for the camera.

One of the best tripods for vlogging remains the small tripods or the "spider" type like the GorillaPods (or another brand, although for quality-price, my recommendation is this specific model).

You can record yourself with these tripods by supporting the camera on almost any surface or using it as an extension while recording in selfie mode. You should choose a model depending on the weight of your camera (or mobile).

Recommended 'spider' tripods: GorillaPod up to 6 and a half lbs., (large cameras, with mirror) and GorillaPod approximately 2 lbs. The other option is the larger one, more traditional tripods. It doesn't have to be a very professional tripod and more expensive than the camera.

Please note that if you have a heavy digital camera, the tripod has to be robust enough to hold it well.

If you are working in the field or mountain, you will require a tripod that can hold up, with an aluminum frame or at least one of not very heavy material, to relieve weight and load as much as possible.

The studio, stage, location or background of the scene to record.

A studio is not a section of the equipment itself. Without a doubt, those who start recording videos for YouTube do not need to have a professional studio. However, when we talk about a recording "studio," this can perfectly be a room with a suitable background and good natural lighting (a window as close as possible to the recording point).

Remember that you can turn a corner of your house into the perfect place to record your videos for very little money.

Having a good space to record your videos is something that can make you stand out from the vast number of YouTubers. So, we are going to see some tips to use the background properly.

Regarding the background or set, we must ensure the focus is centered on the subject and not the background. Separate the person from the background as much as you can physically

Light adds volume and separates the subject from the background. You can also install an additional light source to illuminate the background, for example, from beneath or from aside to cause depth.

You can use objects placed in the studio as a background. But ensure your space is tidy, clean and presentable. It is a turn off to live in a dirt hole or present a bad image to see in the background.

I recommend simply using a white wall area as the background and using a small ambient light next to the wall to break uniformity. However, if you have a little more space and can afford it (it is, really, cheap), buy one of these professional photography backgrounds kits.

Something that looks great is the selective blurring of the background, the bokeh. This is nothing more than a shot where the subject is in focus while the background is out of focus. This effect will give a very cinematic touch to your videos since it is a resource constantly used in the cinema.

Get a good bokeh effect – what do we need?

- Position thesubject as far away from the bottom as possible.

- Use a tele objective lens, which gives us focal length above 50mm to put an approximate figure.

- Use a large-diaphragm aperture.

- If your camera does not have interchangeable lenses or only gives you a kit lens, try to use the largest focal point, the one with the highest zoom, which allows you to frame the scene.

- Move your camera closer to the person as much as the frame you are looking for allows.

- Keep in mind that we want to reduce the depth of field.

If you spend a little and reduce the depth by considerably a lot, any movement of the person will take it out of focus, and the remedy will be worse than the disease. My recommendation is to move the background as far away as possible and play with the depth of field, which offers flexibility.

In cinema productions, marks are made on the floor. It allows the actor to know how far they can move back and forth infilming. If you set camera to autofocus and a very shallow depth of field, your camera may constantly be searching for the perfect focal point, and what it does is a nasty constant blur effect.

There is no need to obsess over blur. It is not worth it if, to achieve this, we have to use a very forced frame that can spoil the final result.

Software to edit your videos – finish your vlog and upload it to the networks.
Finally, once you have the best possible material, you will have to do good editing. Although there are many software and even mobile applications for visual editing, some of the best video editing programs are the following:

- Final Cut Pro X – The best possible video editing program for Apple users.

- Adobe Premiere Pro – The classic cross-platform. Powerful and available for both PC and MAC users.

- DaVinci Resolve – The video editor used in Hollywood.

- CyberLink PowerDirector – A good option for those less experienced in video editing

- Adobe After Effects – Videos with special effects and many options.

- Magisto – The online video editor for Artificial Intelligence.

And that's it. Now it only remains to upload your video to your YouTube channel and continue working to grow your followers and community.

If you follow and take care of the aspects I have told you, your videos will take a huge leap in quality, and I am sure that this will make more and more people see them. Good production quality will increase your YouTube subscriptions and views and even monetize your work in the longer run.

Don't forget that the technical factor is just one factor that will help you grow your subscriber base. Once the necessary equipment to record your videos has been gathered, it only remains, adding the two other ingredients of success: perseverance and creativity.

This is undoubtedly the authentic recipe for success: perseverance and hard work + the right equipment + sublime creativity. Remember that the best equipment in the world is worthless without good ideas to manipulate it. High-end technical equipment will not help you if you do not work hard to get the best out of them.

Now let's come to investing in a proper microphone. You can find a basic guide or have a five-minute conversation with the store manager on camera and other equipment for vlogs. However, information about microphones is hard to get.

Being able to have a good microphone is often more important than even having a powerful video camera since today, many people have an intelligent mobile phone capable of offering more than optimal image quality for streaming channels or video platforms.

Many people already have a good camera to record videos on their mobile phones. However, these latest generation mobiles, or even professional cameras, do not offer such good results when it comes to capturing sound, which is vital if we want our videos to not seem "cheap" and not monotonous.

The kind of microphones I will list in this section are ideal for recording interviews and make cinematic vlogs. They are also excellent value for money as they are usually relatively affordable, at least the "corded" versions.

Of course, we can go for market-leading wireless options like the Sony or Sennheiser tie microphones. Still, if we give up on this convenience, we find offers of microphones capable of recording quality sound at a very reasonable price. Among these options that we discussed with excellent value for money we have the Rode brand and its microphone: Rode Smartlav +

The Rode Smartlav + microphone is ideal for YouTubers who want to record interviews. One of its advantages is its ease of use and portability since it only requires connecting it to a tablet or smartphone through the headphone jack.

For this, the brand provides us with an app, RØDE Rec app for iOS, or another audio application that we want (most mobiles have a native application to record audio). This is undoubtedly one of the most recommended options for its quality-price if you need to buy a microphone for your videos.

Another bestial option for YouTubers is the Shure MOTIV MVL. With this microphone, your videos will take a professional leap. Shure MOTIV MVL is a quick and easy solution for capturing clear audio in digital voice recording, close to the mic.

It also works with any mobile phone or tablet equipped with recording functions, connecting it directly to the headphone jack. It offers its own, high-quality app to start your recordings simply and efficiently.

You also have external microphones for cameras, which is the right way to go. External directional microphones like the Rode VideoMic Pro are possibly the most professional option if you want to dedicate yourself to recording videos. Its great versatility and sound quality make this microphone one of the most used by famous YouTubers, such as YouTube star Casey Neistat.

The Rode Videomic Pro microphone is a directional type, which mainly captures the audio where it is focused at. On the contrary, it records very little the sound of the environment. This achieves results with very little background noise and great clarity. This makes it a specially recommended microphone for YouTubers making outdoor vlogs.

This micro is designed to be placed in the shoe of the camcorder or DSLR camera. Besides, its connector is TRS, so you will not need an adapter (in most professional cameras). Its sound is very clean and of great quality. If you are serious in the world of online video, this is surely your most recommended option.

Tight budget? – Let's look at some best quality-price microphones

If you are on a tight budget and need to buy a simple, practical camera microphone (it does not need a battery, which is very comfortable), and that manages to record audio professionally, I recommend the little brother of the VideoMic Pro: RODE VideoMic.

This microphone has some trimmed features compared to the PRO version, but it also has advantages such as that it already comes with the synthetic hair windshield and that it does not need a battery for its operation.

On the contrary, collect frequencies from 100Hz to 20,000 Hz (the PRO goes from 40Hz to 20kHz), something that you will only notice when recording music or ambient sound, but that practically does not affect the voice. It can even be advantageous to isolate it from unwanted noise and low frequencies.

In summary, if you are looking to buy the best microphone for the price of your camera, you will not find anything better for less price. If you are still not convinced, I recommend you to check videos where practical demos speak of the quality of this microphone and the great professional difference that recording your videos with it makes.

USB microphones for YouTubers

USB microphones are an ideal solution for OFF voice recordings, gameplays, screencast tutorials, gamers, podcasts, etc. The quality offered by any of these models is so good that it is even possible to use them in a professional studio. At least if we want a portable solution that makes it easy for us to move our recording studio anywhere.

Best microphone to record videos from a mobile phone: if you have a state-of-the-art mobile capable of recording equal quality video, you do not need the extra expense of purchasing a professional camera. After all, the price of these cameras is only justified by several options you may never use.

My recommendation is to get professional results from an iPhone or other latest generation mobile phone with a device like Saramonic SmartMixer. This is a two-channel microphone for audio mixing that turns any mobile phone into a professional mini recording studio. It has two microphone inputs, LCD monitor screen, phantom microphone power supply, and amplification for professional studio sound recording. With that being said, this equipment comes with two condenser microphones included.

Without a doubt, a high-quality option that will help you record outdoors, concerts, acoustics, interviews, or take your YouTube vlog to another level.

VIII

Writing vlog scrips that guarantee views

Learn how to write a YouTube script applying neuroscience of selling and copywriting techniques to capture attention, maintain interest, and connect with the emotions of your audience. This chapter explores different tricks on writing vlog scripts.

Here are the tips you need to create scripts using copywriting and neuroscience of selling:

Create a kickass summary
To do this, answer these questions: What is the purpose of the video? Do you want to create a community or enhance your brand? Do you want to advertise or sell a service or product? Are you trying to record a tutorial, instructions, or a training class for your students?

Depending on the objective, the format and the perfect length of the script can vary greatly, as you will see later. What topic are you going to cover? Define what the main idea of the script is and what knowledge you want to transmit to your viewer.

And don't be afraid to be too specific. The more specific your message is, the more you will get with your video.

Who is your target audience?
To attract and activate your client's three brains, you must know in depth what s/he thinks, feels, and needs. Also, both the content and the tone of voice will depend on the audience you are addressing. For example, would you not use the same expressions or words to talk to executives and college students?

What do you want your audience to do (Call-to-Action)?
That is, decide what you want your audience to do after viewing:

To buy?

Share?

To subscribe?

Comment?

Choose the right format

What type of video to choose? Depends on your goal: To sell, create a community, or strengthen your brand, the most effective thing is that you record a personal video where you show your face and talk to the camera. If it is a MasterClass or a step-by-step tutorial, I recommend that you capture the computer screen or the work process (creating crafts or other material works).

In certain cases, a combination of both may be the perfect option. For example, add a small screen where you face and gesture while showing the lesson. Or introduce cuts with diagrams, drawings, or examples in a personal branding advertising video.

Apply a structure with storytelling

Engage the viewer by telling a story like this: Problem = Solution = Benefit = Action

Put on the table a problem, fear, belief, or desire with which your target audience feels identified. Next, present the solution or answer you need and explain how it is going to help you, how it is going to fill a void in your lives. Close the story by giving them the opportunity you just offered. Guide them to action.

Start with the main idea

Make sure to introduce the main idea of the video in the first seconds of the script, otherwise you will lose your audience's attention, and this will end up jumping to the next YouTube video. Summarize the topic you are going to cover in 1 or 2 sentences at the beginning of the script. If you can create an expectation, generate interest so that the audience wants to continue listening to the rest of your story.

Write as if you were talking

Remember that you are not writing an article for your blog. To interact with your audience, write as you speak. Create a script as if you were having a conversation with a friend. Call the viewers, "you."

Introduce questions that make them take sides in the speech. Use expressions typical of the spoken language. Avoid any words that sound strained in your brand voice.

Humor it up

Your script's appropriate amount of humor will vary depending on the type of audience you are targeting and your brand voice. I don't mean that you should laugh out loud with every video. An annoying laugh can kill it. But if you can get the viewer to smile, you will be conquering their emotional limbic system.

Smiling exudes positive emotion; general light and positive demeanor are sexy. Your audience will pick it up from you. And I assure you that, if you connect positively with their feelings, you will leave a mark on their memory. In this way, you will fulfill one of the three keys to the decision-making triangle on which neuroscience of selling is based.

Don't see yourself creating jokes or sweeping smiles with your words? No problem. Remember that we are talking about an audiovisual medium. If the audio is not enough, help yourself with graphic effects: a T-shirt with a witty message, fake shots, animations, adorable pets breaking into the recording (Have you met my cat Prada?)

Create a thorough script

Write everything down. Write as you are going to state the content and add the sections, cuts, and actions that you are going to carry out. This will save you a lot of time during the subsequent recording process.

Take care of the length

In general terms, the shorter your video, the more acceptance it will have from your audience. And, if something is missing for users on the internet, it is time and patience. We live in the age of immediacy. Therefore, the basic rule that you must apply in your video scripts is to reduce and synthesize the content to the maximum.

And to help you, here are some clues depending on the type of script:

Advertising: A duration of 1 to 2 minutes is perfect for capturing attention without wasting time on your audience if it is an advertising video. Considering that the optimal speech speed is about 170-190 words per minute, I recommend writing a short script: 1 or 2 pages.

Training: Our brains' capacity to pay attention in a sustained way does not exceed 15-20 minutes. So, you have two options: Create videos that do not exceed this length by dividing the content into short videos of about 15 minutes, or to insert moments of disconnection within the lesson (examples, videos that break the speech, breaks, invitations to participate).

Personal brand: Although the 15-20-minute rule applies to this type of video, the ideal practice for you is to maintain a trend. The reptilian brain likes patterns, feels comfortable and safe in routines. Determine how long you feel comfortable and keep that format in all your scripts. 1 minute? 5? 10? Your choice, but be consistent.

Practice

Do you have your script ready?

Recite it out loud just as you would in the final recording. This will help you eliminate or replace those fragments that do not sound natural in a conversation and give you the security you need in front of the camera.

Rehearse several times until you are familiar with the text, and a natural speech comes out. Pay attention to your words or words of support and try to avoid them: mmm ..., uh ...

Recording and viewing these tests can help you identify postures, gestures, failures, or hobbies that you prefer to polish or avoid. With practice, you will gain experience, and it will cost you less and less to obtain results that you feel proud of.

Love yourself

To give value to your followers, you need to take care of yourself: You are your worst critic.

I know that you are afraid to expose yourself to the public and that you will be a little ashamed of your first videos. But remember, we've all been through that first time, we've all felt that way. And it will be an experience that helps you improve.

To get to video 10, you must start with number 1. Go ahead! The only opinion that counts is yours. Humans are passionate and very diverse people. It is impossible to please everyone. If you follow these key steps, you will fall in love with your ideal viewer. However, you are likely to get an opposite reaction from other people.

Think coldly: if you target a specific audience, why should you be affected by the opinion of an audience that does not interest you?

Do you get criticism? Objectively analyze comments, use constructive advice or ideas to grow and improve with practice, eliminate and forget the malicious ones.

When someone criticizes out of hatred, they are projecting their problems onto you. Do not be fooled. The problem is with them.

Do you have a troll? First, rejoice. That means your videos are gaining followers. And second, DON'T FEED IT. Ignore it, avoid answering. That would only allow them to continue attacking you.

Starting a YouTube channel, you must consider costs involved, equipment, and other variables.

As it happens, I took the challenge of creating a Video studio to create YouTube content in the previous chapter.

"I live in New York; how can I afford all this?"

I thought of a Video studio "on a tight budget," but didn't have specific figures in mind. I set out to put together a guide that would let us create top-notch quality videos but without emptying pockets.

So, let's take a walk through the process. Steps to set up a studio for your YouTube channel in the most economical way possible:

We will try to find the minimum configuration that gives us an acceptable quality and spend the least possible money. For this, one of the first things we will do is avoid buying anything unnecessary, or that does not have a large impact on the results.

The camera is the first step. Many of us nowadays have mobiles capable of recording 4K video. If this is the case, think that you already have practically half of what you need to start recording your videos, and you still would not have spent a single dollar.

But let's go step by step.

Think about the type of content you are going to record. The first thing to consider is what type of content you want to make. This particular set of YouTube Studio is designed to "talk" about explanatory, informative, or product videos in which a person is talking to the camera. The subject will be built up gradually.

This will be an "A-Roll" production, widens up as it proceeds. The "B-Roll" footage supporting what is said will be created separately or taken from other sources.

We can also use this same space to demonstrate things. However, screen or press recordings will commonly be used, as well as scenes filmed abroad. Although what I am going to teach you below can be an important starting point for your videos.

Keep in mind that you will need to think carefully about how your content style will affect the decisions you make about what equipment to get and how to configure it.

Now let's go with the first fundamental element to record quality videos:

The camera

It may seem that it is the most important factor at first, but it is not. If you want to save money, even start recording your videos for free, look at your mobile first. Today even mid-range mobiles are already capable of recording 4K videos, and you can get good image quality with these cameras and a tripod.

If you already have a mobile or a camera that records with decent quality at FHD or 4K, do the math. Think if, before investing in a better camera, you could improve the lighting and sound of your videos for a lower cost.

Audio is very important. I cannot stress this enough.

Audio is one of the tricky areas.

Viewers will be okay with the imperfect video quality. But few things will affect someone moving to another video more than bad sound. There are two variables to this problem. One is the background, and the other is the microphone.

The microphone. The cheapest option to improve your video.

There are many options for microphones, ranging from few dollars to thousands. Luckily to start recording your videos, you are going to need a type of microphone that is quite accessible and inexpensive:

The lapel microphones.

You can use two options: a wired or wireless lapel microphone. We choose the second option. But if you want to adjust your budget, you can find one with cable for about $15-20 and get great results.

The advantage of lavalier microphones is that they do not pick up the distant sound too loudly. They are programmed to collect your voice and isolate it from all that that happens outside your space

Of course, you can use a microphone on an off-camera mount (or on-camera, your choice), but be aware that each type of microphone has its pros and cons. Pole microphones are also an option, but they tend to pick up more noise from the room.

Acoustic treatment of the room; zero cost.

I don't propose a soundproof room. It is a massive and expensive task that we can save by simply using microphones that do not capture too much external noise and editing the subjects or filming when things are calmer.

The background setting of the room is important. Specifically, when it comes to reflectance or echoes. It is when the sound originating from a source bounces around the space. The best way to reduce this is to throw some soft materials in the room: sofas, curtains, chairs, cushions and the like. Making videos in an empty room will create echo louder than your voice.

TRICK...

The more dense and padded elements your room has, the fewer vibrations and bounces of sounds you will have. That is why radio jockeys conduct shows in closet spaced studios. The background absorbs all the reverb, making the sound of the recording very dry.

You don't want to kill the reflection completely, because going too far otherwise can make recordings sound lifeless. In my case, the room has a green screen at one end, a closed wood at the other, and a carpet.

Reflectance was a problem between the two bare walls next door. The solution I used was to hang two thick curtains on each side outside the shot. This reduces the reflected sound.

As you can see, you can get a decent acoustic treatment without spending any money, simply rearranging your room where you are going to record.

Lighting to record videos at a pro-level with little money

Another of the most important factors to get a material that looks professional is lighting. Even if your camera is not too good, if it illuminates the subject well, it will look great. Even the best cameras can't fix poor lighting.

Lighting is more important than the quality of your camera, and it is also usually cheaper. Three-point lighting is the standard for lighting a subject correctly. You need a key (main) light, a backlight, and a fill light.

You can also use small LED lights or lamps in the background of the scene to give your videos a little more personality and personal style.

A professional setup would be: First Spotlight illuminates the subject from above. The two main lights fill the space with diffuse lights, and then the final LED light is used to remove some unwanted shadows resulting from the two main lights shining on the subject.

You will have to adapt the lighting to the available space.

Buying a normal three-point lighting kit is fine to start with, but you may notice that more may be necessary for your study space. You will think that this type of lighting is very expensive for your budget, but you can find quite decent equipment for less than $100.

Even if your budget is very tight and you cannot afford to buy additional light bulbs, you can use the natural light from a large window, the lamps you have in your house to fill, and a background. Natural light is always a good option when shooting videos!

A tripod: Basic and Cheap.

Most available cameras or mobile tripods under $100 should suffice. Somewhere in Amazon's $25-55 zone, you will find a nice sturdy tripod ideal for indoor home use. Check the best sellers, and generally, you will find a perfect tripod in that affordable price range.

There are several tripods available for mobiles. However, for this stage, one of the octopus-type tripods with flexible legs capable of "mounting anywhere" can solve many ballots. They will allow you to fix your smartphone to walls, doors, pipes, etc.

For a secondary camera, this is a great option too.

Video editing

We have already discussed the best video editors for YouTube. If our budget is tight, we are going to want to use the money available in equipment rather than in software. That is why we recommend using free edition programs on our computer, laptop, or in an app for our mobile or tablet.

If you use Mac systems, the choice is clear, iMovie is free and easy to use. It will also familiarize you with what, for many, is the best video editing program: Final Cut. If you use a PC, you must get Adobe Premiere Pro.

You can also try more advanced programs like DaVinci Resolve: a program used even in some Hollywood movies and which is free for non-commercial editions.

Last conclusions

I've shown you a cheap and homemade setup. With a small investment and a little effort, you can make videos that reflect greater attention to detail. They can also produce a greater viewing experience for your viewers.

Of course, these are just the rough tools you need. Most of the work is done with other parts of the workflow, such as the script, editing, and actual performance of the camera itself. Even the most professional YouTube studio can't make you a better content creator, and the best content creators can do something compelling with the essentials.

"I want to do it right. What YouTube mistakes should I avoid?"

Well, today is your lucky day, because although I do not have a YouTube channel, I have learned a lot in recent times from my perspective, as well as thanks to the analysis or comments of other YouTubers.

But first, let me tell you a little bit why I decided to create this section with YouTube errors that you should avoid.

I am going to start with most people's experience. A lot of people have started as YouTubers recently. The process takes a long time. Most people are those YouTubers that take the time to sit in front of the camera and start recording.

They think if they had started much earlier, their channel would be bigger. Their YouTube income could be higher, and obviously, they would have learned many more things. Today, I want to show you, in my opinion, that I consider the 10 YouTube errors that you should avoid starting off on the right foot.

Never being ready for it

This, for me, has been the most serious mistake people make. They spend so much time watching other YouTubers, researching the equipment they had, what microphone they used or what camera was the ideal one. Then in the end, time passed, and their channel was still there waiting.

If you want good advice, start today with what you have.

If you have a decent phone, start making your videos, even if it is to practice and try things or until you get used to "acting" in front of the camera (something that is not easy for everyone) THERE'S NOTHING WRONG WITH GETTING BETTER WITH TIME.

What's more, there is nothing wrong with going on the go, improving and practicing. It will even help you improve your level of video editing. But do not wait to have the best camera, the best microphone, or be the genius of video editing to start with your YouTube channel.

Do not make this mistake on YouTube that cost people dearly. Don't be the person with three tripods, four microphones, two cameras, and several knick-knacks to film.

Neglecting audio

Among the YouTube mistakes that many make is worrying more about the image than the audio. It is a serious error. People can bear that a video looks bad (think that in many countries, because of the Internet, YouTube does not load more than 360p), but people will not hold a video that the audio is heard badly.

Even to me, when I see a video, it does not matter that it has been uploaded in 1080p60fps. If the sound is bad, it produces that "I don't know what" that makes me want to quit it, however interesting it may be.

Not knowing what your niche is

This is one of the YouTube errors that I have seen the most in many YouTubers that have very good content but cannot succeed with their channel. What is it about? Practically not knowing what type of channel to handle or which niche to target.

You can see YouTubers who suddenly make tutorials, then make funny videos, and also have gameplays of games and what not, reviews of programs or applications. In the end, their channel looks like a salad that doesn't make any sense, and people don't know whether to subscribe or not.

So, my advice at this point is to analyze well what audience you want to reach with what kind of themes or content and try to improve in that area. Don't be the jack of all trades. And not everything should be home or street jokes.

I say this because it seems lately that you can only be a YouTuber playing pranks on others.

Trying too hard for perfection

If you are looking for the first videos of great YouTubers, you will see that their first videos were not a big deal in relation to the videos they upload now. I would even dare to say that they did not have the best audio or image.

But does it matter? What matters is starting.

This is yet another of the YouTube mistakes: to worry about the video being perfect. And the truth is that you will never end completely convinced, even if your audience loves it.

Take my advice: create videos, test, edit, upload them, be on the record, don't worry about it being the best video in the world, at least for now. The perfect video doesn't exist, so don't let this stop you.

Not having your style

In the life of the YouTuber, there is everything, but what stands out the most is that style or personal touch that you give to your videos. I have seen very creative YouTubers, including others who copy the style of some famous people.

You should sit down and think about how you would like that style to be, what feeling you want to convey and create that character.

YouTube is like being in a movie, and having a good character is worth a lot.

I'm not asking you to be an Oscar-worthy actor either but try to create an essence. You can use certain phrases, a way of introducing yourself, or even a fun or relaxed style that comes to mind. But don't make the mistake of being too serious or looking like a zombie talking to the camera. Do not be Logan Paul, either. There are people out there who want to have a connection with you, and that style is the key.

Believing YouTube is everything

Beware of this error.

And it is one of those YouTube mistakes that almost everyone makes. By this I mean just using YouTube and waiting for the magic to happen. No, it is not like that.

Success on YouTube is complemented by a good strategy of presence on social networks and other media platforms. Many YouTubers usually complement the dissemination of their videos with other tools or social networks, and this is something great because that way, your channel will grow.

Copying other creators

If you keep following around what PewDiePie does and how he addresses his audio, you would be a PewDiePie BETA, and nobody wants that. The audience is picky and can detect when you are copying others.

The first impression is the last impression.

Do not copy another YouTuber. Your audience will flag you, and it's a creepy move. It makes you look insecure. Uncomfortable in your skin. Desperate for success. Remember, a good impression is set by originality and bringing forward your own creation.

Moreover, not everything works for anyone. If you believe that trolling the public or using Internet jargon is the way to go because it's the ultimate secret to engaging your audience, then you are wrong. It's all about trial and error. Do not overdo anything.

Expecting overnight results

Success will not knock your door instantly. It's not an Amazon same-day delivery. A YouTube channel is like a small business. You have to push above your weight to succeed. Building an audience, setting an impression, making the algorithm work in your favor, creating and editing videos, and working at the backend takes a chunk of effort and time.

Results do not come instantly. A video will be uploaded, circulated on the web. It must be marketed. It has to stay on the web. When you start, you face a heap of odds at your disposal. Consistency pushes those odds away. It would take some time before you start seeing results. There's also competition. Remember my point: someone in your niche doing a better job would be present. But that does not mean you need to see the exit door. It's not about who's doing the better or worst job. It's about doing a good job and doing it every day.

"I want to beat my competition out of business."

Beating the competition is not an easy task, but it is important for YouTubers with high aspirations. There are always competitors. If you don't find them because you created a new product, they will appear as soon as it is validated in the market. How many are there in the tech sector? JerryRightEverything, Marques Brownlee, Unbox Therapy, iJustine, and so many others. Heck, PewDiePie vs. T-series.

In this section, I am going to give you some guidelines, so you know how to beat your competition and steal away their viewers. Divert viewers from their channel to yours. Although in reality, it is not so much a fight but rather an exercise in attracting viewers. You have to convince viewers to click on your videos rather than others'. Aim to do a better job than others.

Know the strengths and weaknesses of your value proposition

It is the fundamental starting point of any channel. How will you outperform your competition if you don't know what the comparative advantages your value proposition has?

Keep in mind that you will have to be very objective. It is very easy for a creator to fall in love with their own project and believe that they are better than others in everything. However, this is rarely the case. Review aspects such as quality, design, production, content, brand image, etc. Also remember the words of Jack Welch, former president of General Electric: " If you don't have a competitive advantage, don't compete. "

By that, I don't mean that you abandon your project, but to reinforce it, and look for alternatives. Have a different touch to it. I named so many YouTubers in the tech sector above. They all do more or less the same thing. But somehow, they are different. They all have their unique styles of presentation.

So, it is important to analyze your value proposition and even test it before launching your project.

Analyze your competition

If we talk about knowing what the competitive advantages of your channel are, by definition, you have to be able to compare yourself with the competition. That makes it essential that you analyze your main competitors.

You will have to list down the main criteria that motivates the purchase decision of your customers and try to analyze it objectively for each of the main competitors. In some sectors, it is very easy, because all the information is publicly available. In others, it is more difficult to know the details of the strategies.

Know your audience very well

As I said in the introduction, the goal is not knowing how to beat the competition, but rather how to seduce the viewer, and to convince them to prefer your value proposition. For this, it is essential to study the profile of your audience, especially as to what motivates their decision to watch your videos.

I'm going to put an example—the market for gaming videos. If you limited yourself to analyzing the competition, you would immediately realize that YouTube is saturated with such content.

One conclusion could be: "I am going to make unique content, so I can have all the attention."
Error; different channels have tried and failed. Why? Because customers associate familiarity
and quality. They believe that videos are good because they care about what they are looking for.
And really, uniqueness in this regard doesn't work. If you enter the market ignoring this
information, you will probably fail.

Draw a differentiation strategy
Now you should know the strong points of your project. You also know what your audience
wants and values. And you have analyzed the offer of your competition. The logical conclusion
is that you can establish a differentiation strategy.

In other words, you are going to insist on the strengths you have, your comparative advantages,
and especially on those points that the audience values the most.

This differentiation strategy must be present in all stages of the marketing of your channel. Of
course, it will be a part of your communication and the discourse of the production, but you also
must think about the presentation of the brand, the design of the videos, your role in them, etc.

Commitment to innovation
To innovate is to do things differently. It does not necessarily have to be a technological
improvement. Things as simple (in appearance) as simplifying a process or offering an additional
service can represent a greater value contribution for the audience. So, do not hesitate, and bet on
innovation.

Adapt your value proposition to the evolution of the market
A YouTube channel has to evolve its value proposition, and in some cases, even its production
model. Even if you manage to become the leader, you cannot assume that the strategy that has
brought you to the top will serve you forever. Trends change. Competitors adapt. New players
appear. If you're not careful, the same thing can happen.

Esmée Denters is nowhere there. Ray William-Johnson decided to delve into rapping, and his
song only managed to gain a few hundred thousand views. Where is Britanni Louise Taylor? Has
anyone heard from Tyler Oakley lately?

Loyalty to your viewers
One of the best ways to prevent your customers from leaving is to have loyalty. There are many
ways to achieve this. A supermarket creates a discount or even a financing card. Amazon offers a

monthly subscription that saves you shipping costs, and therefore encourages you to buy more. Apple has an ecosystem that is incompatible with other brands, making it much more difficult to go to the competition.

Yes, you're not a multi-billion-dollar LLC. But viewers are the same. Eventually, they are customers, and you must treat them like customers.

In general, the best loyalty strategy is to offer great service and satisfy the customer. But completing it with some additional technique is a very good idea. Offer coupon codes. Offer percentage discounts to popular services with a special promo code. You can do so much.

Have adapted communication

To beat your competition, you also have to bet on communication. In this case, we are already talking about more subjective aspects. Marketing and tools like storytelling allow you to create a speech and an emotion around your brand or products you are selling through YouTube.

If you are successful in your communication, you can significantly reinforce the audience's minds and strengths of your value proposition, which is a great advantage.

Do not speak ill of your competitors

It is an aspect that I wanted to highlight because sometimes YouTubers are wrong about it. There's an area of YouTube where creators are in an actual war. They are all *Karens* of YouTube.

Knowing how to beat the competition doesn't mean talking bad about it. There are several reasons for this. The first is ethical. That is not a dirty war. The second is that it is very bad to speak disparagingly of your competitors.

Customers are not dumb. They will probably get a bad opinion of you and your channel if you do. Finally, you have to know what you tell your audience. Your competitor will most likely end up knowing, and there is no point in alienating abusive criticism.

Therefore, we always insist on the good side. Do not speak ill of what the competition offers. It is not the same to say that your value proposition is better than to say that theirs is worse. The nuance is very important.

How to beat the competition when they are investing more and more to lure the audience?

I couldn't finish a post on how to beat the competition without talking about a classic: the price war. On YouTube, certain creators go the extra mile of engaging their audience by offering them too good to be true deals. They can do it. But you, as a novice YouTuber, would not.

However, if you do the same, chances are everyone will lose, and then it will cost a lot to go back to it. A trend would set. The audience gets used to it fast. So, what can you do?

Reinforce your value proposition. Imagine that a competitor with content having characteristics very similar to yours decides to offer ridiculous promotions to get subscribers. The implicit message that it sends to consumers is the following: "This offer is already something basic (a commodity), and whoever pays more is stupid."

If you don't want to do the same, you must reinforce the audience's perception of value. That implies designing new functionalities and content that the audience can appreciate and incorporate them into the value proposition.

You must sell the added value of your content. Analytics is the first line with the audience. You will likely be able to convince viewers if you know how to highlight the comparative advantages of your content.

Of course, you have two requirements. One is obviously to reinvent your content so that they know the reinforced value proposition well (point one).

The second point is that you choose the profile of your ads well. We are all different. Some of us decided more for the price, others more for the value—marketing and branding work. As I have said before, communication is a key element of differentiation.

If you want to beat your competition when you have this war, you have to redesign your communication. You will include the new features and services, and you will bet on generating a quality image, with added value.

With these tips, you can see that beating your competitors is not an easy task. It requires a lot of analysis work and permanent adaptation. But it works. Too many creators do not give it the necessary importance. Do not make the same mistake.

<u>Afterthoughts</u>

We have now reached an end to this eBook. It was an absolute privilege to prepare this. I want to thank my dog, Ollie, for staring at me all the time and *arf!* for the little doggo treats.

This book got me traveling to places, meeting, and sitting down with multiple people from the YouTube Creators Academy and getting word from them. This book is dedicated to every Content Creator out there set to make a difference, create value, and aim for success in the realm of YouTube.

It is most certainly the easiest platform of all. It presents a full suite of opportunities. All you need is to pay attention and do what you love every day.

Remember that there will be days when you will continue to question why you are doing this. There will be endless evenings where you are intimidated by people who are doing it with perfect finesse and collecting thousands of dollars in checks.

However, take the influence as a push to work harder and do a better job than them. You are capable of doing it better. You just need to start doing. Likewise, this eBook did not carry a magic recipe. By the time you finished, you did not spawn an out-of-this-world resource that put you ten steps ahead of everyone.

This is your Bible for YouTube. Revisit it. Reread chapters. Take a few months and then read it again.

Good luck.

****

"If you have enjoyed reading this book, I would be very grateful if you could post an honest review. All that you need to do is to click here, then click the blue link next to the yellow stars. On the left, You'll see a gray button that says "Write a customer review"—click that and you're good to go, thank you."

Donall

www.ingramcontent.com/pod-product-compliance
Lightning Source LLC
Chambersburg PA
CBHW050125240326
41458CB00122B/1409

9 781777 330453